THIS BOOK BELONGS TO

_____

START DATE

_____

SHE READS TRUTH

EXECUTIVE

FOUNDER/CHIEF EXECUTIVE OFFICER
Raechel Myers

CO-FOUNDER/CHIEF CONTENT OFFICER
Amanda Bible Williams

CHIEF OPERATING OFFICER
Ryan Myers

ASSISTANT TO THE EXECUTIVES
Taura Ryan

EDITORIAL

EDITORIAL DIRECTOR
Jessica Lamb

MANAGING EDITOR
Beth Joseph, MDiv

DIGITAL MANAGING EDITOR
Oghosa Iyamu, MDiv

ASSOCIATE EDITORS
Lindsey Jacobi, MDiv
Tameshia Williams, ThM

EDITORIAL ASSISTANT
Hannah Little, MTS

MARKETING

CUSTOMER JOURNEY
MARKETING MANAGER
Megan Gibbs

PRODUCT MARKETING MANAGER
Wesley Chandler

SOCIAL MEDIA STRATEGIST
Taylor Krupp

CREATIVE

CREATIVE DIRECTOR
Amy Dennis

ART DIRECTORS
Kelsea Allen
Aimee Lindamood

DESIGNERS
Abbey Benson
Amanda Brush, MA
Annie Glover
Lauren Haag

OPERATIONS

OFFICE MANAGER
Nicole Quirion

PROJECT ASSISTANT
Mary Beth Montgomery

SHIPPING

SHIPPING MANAGER
Elizabeth Thomas

FULFILLMENT LEAD
Cait Baggerman

FULFILLMENT SPECIALISTS
Kajsa Matheny
Ashley Richardson
Noe Sanchez

SUBSCRIPTION INQUIRIES
orders@shereadstruth.com

COMMUNITY SUPPORT

COMMUNITY SUPPORT MANAGER
Kara Hewett, MOL

COMMUNITY SUPPORT SPECIALISTS
Katy McKnight
Heather Vollono
Margot Williams

CONTRIBUTORS

SPECIAL THANKS
Lauren Gloyne
Neely Tabor

@SHEREADSTRUTH

Download the
She Reads Truth app,
available for iOS
and Android

Subscribe to the
She Reads Truth podcast

SHEREADSTRUTH.COM

SHE READS TRUTH™

© 2022 by She Reads Truth, LLC

All rights reserved.

All photography used by permission.

ISBN 978-1-952670-59-6

1 2 3 4 5 6 7 8 9 10

All Scripture is taken from the Christian Standard Bible®. Copyright © 2020 by Holman Bible Publishers. Used by permission. Christian Standard Bible® and CSB® are federally registered trademarks of Holman Bible Publishers.

Though the dates in this book have been carefully researched, scholars disagree on the dating of many biblical events.

Research support provided by Logos Bible Software™. Learn more at logos.com.

AMEN AND AMEN

A JOURNEY THROUGH THE PSALMS

SHE READS TRUTH

This book tells a
redemption story.

Jessica

Jessica Lamb
EDITORIAL DIRECTOR

After years of anticipation, I sat in a theater waiting to see my favorite musical on stage. When the lights dimmed, the orchestra began to play, and the baritone began to sing the opening lyrics, I burst into tears. My cheeks stayed damp for the next two hours and forty-five minutes. It didn't matter that I'd heard the words so often I could have sung along. It didn't matter that I knew the story backwards and forwards. When it was over, I stood up to applaud until my hands hurt.

In this show, each character is represented by a short, recurring musical moment. At the end, these motifs layer onto one another in a scene full of energy and complex emotion. Each individual song is powerful on its own. But only in witnessing the entire story is the artistry of the whole composition fully understood.

The book of Psalms is organized in a similar way. The larger book is structured as five smaller units, each made up of individual songs and poems. Many of us have never read the Psalms as an entire collection. More often, we read favorite psalms or look at them in literary groups. There's certainly nothing wrong with this approach (we've done it as a She Reads Truth community and loved it!). But in doing so exclusively, we can miss the artistry of the whole collection.

In this reading plan, we'll look at psalms from each of the five books to build a framework for understanding the book of Psalms as a whole. We'll see how this book tells a redemption story—one of a mighty, powerful God who drew near to broken humanity, who promised an eternal King, and who remains the same from generation to generation. Each psalm also reminds us that God meets us in whatever state we're in—in our loneliness, sorrow, and celebration (see the "Emotion in Psalms" extra on page 78).

Our stories, just like the people who wrote each psalm, are not the whole story. But they are part of God's grand redemption. Through these Holy Spirit-inspired words, we're reminded that there is hope when everything seems lost, life when death and decay seem to press in, and community and purpose when all we see is loneliness and fear.

Our title comes from a refrain that occurs three times in Psalms. *Amen* is a Hebrew affirmation, a confident declaration that what was previously stated is the truth. It can be translated as, "Let it be so!," "Certainly!," "Surely!," "Truly!," or, my personal archaic favorite, "Verily!" Our prayer is that as you learn to read the Psalms book by book, you would join those who have gone before us by responding to God's faithful redemption with a bold, declarative, "Amen and amen!"

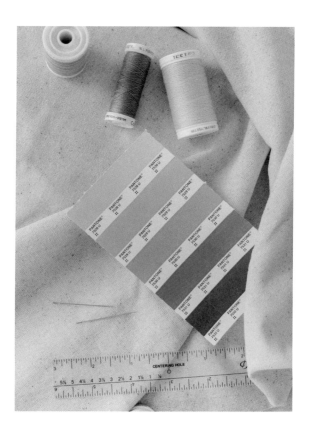

At She Reads Truth, we believe in pairing the inherently beautiful Word of God with the aesthetic beauty it deserves. Each of our resources is thoughtfully and artfully designed to highlight the beauty, goodness, and truth of Scripture in a way that reflects the themes of each curated reading plan.

While designing this Study Book, we were inspired by the intricate beauty of woven textiles. Our team created hand-sewn unique geometric patterns on Bristol board. These textile elements are featured throughout the book, reminding us that each individual psalm is but a stitch in the tapestry. One of our favorites is on the cover—the gradient stitching creates five distinct sections, pointing us back to the five books of the Psalms.

The photographs selected for this book have a quiet, contemplative tone and feature stitching that runs throughout the book. The fonts have a balance of angular features and calligraphic loops to highlight the range of emotions and themes experienced in the Psalms.

The color palette is inspired by the muted hues of an antique rug, calling to mind the journey of a life with God—its highs and lows and well-worn places within the greater design.

HOW TO USE THIS BOOK

She Reads Truth is a community of women dedicated to reading the Word of God every day. In the **Amen and Amen** reading plan, we will read selected psalms from each of the five "books," or sections, that make up the book of Psalms to see how each section contributes to the overall message of the Psalms.

READ & REFLECT

Your **Amen and Amen** Study Book focuses primarily on Scripture, with bonus resources to facilitate deeper engagement with God's Word.

SCRIPTURE READING

Designed for a Monday start, this Study Book presents selected psalms from each section of Psalms in daily readings.

REFLECTION

Each weekday and section feature space for personal reflection.

COMMUNITY & CONVERSATION

You can start reading this book at any time! If you want to join women from Jefferson City to Jersey as they read along with you, the She Reads Truth community will start Day 1 of **Amen and Amen** on Monday, August 22, 2022.

 SHE READS TRUTH APP

Devotionals corresponding to each daily reading can be found in the **Amen and Amen** reading plan on the She Reads Truth app. New devotionals will be published each weekday once the plan begins on Monday, August 22, 2022. You can use the app to participate in community discussion, download free lock screens for Weekly Truth memorization, and more.

GRACE DAY

Use Saturdays to catch up on your reading, pray, and rest in the presence of the Lord.

WEEKLY TRUTH

Sundays are set aside for Scripture memorization.

See tips for memorizing Scripture on page 144.

EXTRAS

This book features additional tools to help you gain a deeper understanding of the text.

Find a complete list of extras on page 11.

 SHEREADSTRUTH.COM

The **Amen and Amen** reading plan and devotionals will also be available at SheReadsTruth.com as the community reads each day. Invite your family, friends, and neighbors to read along with you!

 SHE READS TRUTH PODCAST

Subscribe to the She Reads Truth podcast and join our founders and their guests each week as they talk about the beauty, goodness, and truth they find in Scripture.

 Podcast episodes 142–144 for our **Amen and Amen** *series release on Mondays beginning August 22, 2022.*

Table of Contents

BOOK

BOOK

V

Extras

Anonymous

"Life Is but a Weaving"

My life is but a weaving, between my God and me,

I do not choose the colors, He worketh steadily,

Oftimes He weaveth sorrow, and I in foolish pride,

Forget He sees the upper, and I the under side.

Not till the loom is silent, and shuttles cease to fly,

Will God unroll the canvas and explain the reason why.

The dark threads are as needful in the skillful Weaver's hand,

As the threads of gold and silver in the pattern He has planned.

KEY PASSAGE

I waited patiently for the L<small>ORD</small>,
and he turned to me and heard
   my cry for help.
He brought me up from a desolate pit,
out of the muddy clay,
and set my feet on a rock,
making my steps secure.
He put a new song in my mouth,
a hymn of praise to our God.
Many will see and fear,
and they will trust in the L<small>ORD</small>.

PSALM 40:1–3

Reading Psalms
by the Book

1

A LITTLE BACKGROUND

The book of Psalms is a collection of psalms (hymns, songs, or prayers). The Psalter (another name for the book of Psalms) is one large book made up of five smaller books. In total, it consists of 150 psalms composed by individuals or groups from the time of Moses (fifteenth century BC) to a time following the exile (sixth century BC or later). Almost half of the psalms are marked as being "of David," which likely means they were written by King David.

These different psalms were collected, curated, and arranged by editors after the Babylonian exile. The editors divided these psalms into five books, or subdivisions, to tell a cohesive story that reflects the history of Israel. The themes, literary forms, and unique characteristics of each individual psalm give shape to the message of each one of these five books and contribute to the broader message of the whole.

2

THE FIVE BOOKS

The first two books follow the story of David and his royal family, from David's trust in God to establish his throne to a celebration of the Davidic line and God's presence in the temple. The third book explores the downward spiral of David's descendants and the subsequent tragedy of the exile. The fourth emphasizes God's sovereignty and reign, placing Israel's season of exile in the context of God's eternal kingdom. The fifth and final book invites all people to praise God because of His covenant faithfulness, while anticipating the day the promise of a forever King from David's line would be fulfilled in the Messiah.

3

MESSAGE & PURPOSE

The book of Psalms is deeply relational, curated for past, present, and future worshipers. They give us a window into who God is, how He acts, and how His people can respond to Him. Like us, the psalmists looked forward to a day when they would see the King of kings reign forever and where they would live in the fullness of God's presence.

This record of how God's people responded in worship and prayer teaches us how to seek God in every circumstance of life as we wait for Christ's return. The book of Psalms points us to God's authority and His goodness, instilling in those who trust in Him a confidence that He will be faithful to His promises.

4

READING PSALMS BY THE BOOK

In this reading plan we will explore the book of Psalms, reading a selection from each smaller book that represents the narrative and thematic arc of each section.

Reading the book of Psalms through the lens of these five books lifts our eyes to the overall themes and patterns of the whole collection, not just the beauty and emotion of each individual psalm. It helps us anchor our individual and corporate worship in both the legacy and future hope of our faith. This approach will give us a framework for our future reading of the Psalter as we gain a broader understanding of the book as a whole.

Tips for
Reading Psalms

1

READ EACH PSALM IN LIGHT OF THE AUTHOR'S CIRCUMSTANCE.

The psalms are not meant to be read as detached poetry—each one has connections to certain times, people, or places. Let the original application and intent inform present application.

2

READ EACH PSALM IN LIGHT OF ITS BROADER CONTEXT.

Read each psalm in its entirety, keeping in view the broader book and the entire Bible.

3

LOOK FOR METAPHORS, IMAGERY, AND OTHER PATTERNS IN EACH PSALM.

Many literary and poetic devices are used throughout the book of Psalms. These devices help communicate literal truth through abstract language, symbols, and style.

See "Poetic Devices in Scripture" on page 20.

4

NOTICE HOW GOD IS DESCRIBED.

The book of Psalms informs what we know about God's power, character, and interactions with humanity. As you read, look to be reminded of who God is and how we can respond to Him.

5

NOTICE HOW THE PSALMS REVEAL OUR NEED.

In the Psalter there is a repeated longing for redemption and restoration. The bleak language and imagery point toward the ultimate hope and fulfillment of these desires, Jesus Christ.

6

ALLOW YOURSELF TO BE SHAPED BY THE PSALMS.

The psalms have served as both prayers and songs of worship for the people of God for thousands of years. Praying and singing the psalms allows us to develop new vocabulary in our conversations with God.

Poetic Devices
in Scripture

The book of Psalms is a collection of Hebrew poetry. As such, psalms use meter, form, and abstract language to communicate truth that can be difficult to express in plain speech or language. Poetic language invites us to consider complex ideas from an imaginative and emotive perspective.

Here are some examples of literary devices in Hebrew poetry.

ACROSTIC

A poem where the first letter of each line forms a word, phrase, or pattern in the original language.

PS 145

APOSTROPHE

An address to an absent subject as though they were present.

PS 148

CHIASM

A form of parallelism that organizes a series of ideas, narratives, phrases, or sections in a mirrored pattern, presenting thoughts then repeating them in reverse order.

PS 90

HYPERBOLE

An intentional exaggeration for increased effect.

PS 42:3

METAPHOR

A figure of speech that states one subject is another for comparison.

PS 23:1

PARALLELISM

The repetition of similar words, phrases, or ideas in multiple lines. Sometimes an idea is repeated in new terms, expounded on more specifically, or countered to add emphasis to an idea.

PS 27:1

PERSONIFICATION

Assigning human attributes to nonhuman things, events, or God.

PS 43:3

SIMILE

An explicit comparison between two concepts.

PS 1:3

BOOK

I

Psalms 1–41

INTRODUCTION

Book I opens with two psalms that declare the reign of God and the value of His law. These psalms act as an introduction to the entire book of Psalms, establishing the major themes the Psalter explores. Book I concludes with a personal lament, grieving betrayal while still trusting in the God of Israel. All but four of the psalms in this first book are attributed to David. In David's psalms, he expressed his longing for the presence of God as well as his hope and trust that the Lord would deliver him from his many enemies and establish his throne.

The personal nature of the psalms in Book I demonstrates that all those who place their hope and trust in the Lord, aligning their lives with His kingdom, can rest in His deliverance.

/\

KEY FACTS

1 Thirty-seven psalms in this section are attributed to David, a shepherd from Bethlehem who became the second king of Israel. David was a musician in Saul's court (1Sm 16:14–23) and as king displayed an interest in sacred music (2Ch 7:6; 23:18). His experience as a shepherd likely informed his reflection on the character of God in Psalm 23.

2 These psalms primarily use the name *Yahweh* for God. Yahweh is the intimate, covenantal, relational name of God. In most English Bibles, this name for God is shown in translation as "Lord."

3 Matthew 27:46 records Jesus echoing the words of Psalm 22 on the cross.

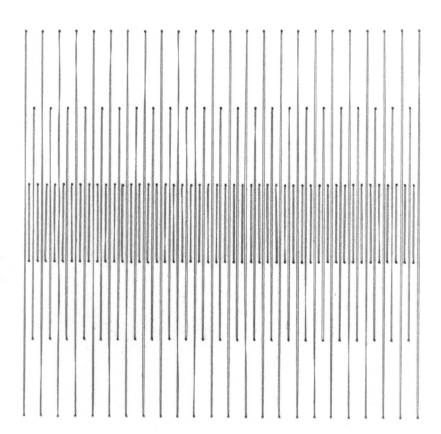

His delight is in the Lᴏʀᴅ's instruction,
and he meditates on it day and night.

PSALM 1:2

Delight in God

Throughout your reading, brief statements will help remind you of the framework of the broader book.

PSALMS 1–2

———

The Psalter opens with an emphasis on God's Word and reign.

PSALM 1

THE TWO WAYS

1 How happy is the one who does not
   walk in the advice of the wicked
   or stand in the pathway with sinners
   or sit in the company of mockers!
2 Instead, his delight is in the LORD's instruction,
   and he meditates on it day and night.
3 He is like a tree planted beside flowing streams
   that bears its fruit in its season,
   and its leaf does not wither.
   Whatever he does prospers.

4 The wicked are not like this;
   instead, they are like chaff that the wind blows away.
5 Therefore the wicked will not stand up in the judgment,
   nor sinners in the assembly of the righteous.

6 For the LORD watches over the way of the righteous,
   but the way of the wicked leads to ruin.

I always let the LORD guide me.
Because he is at my right hand,
I will not be shaken.

PSALM 16:8

PSALM 2

CORONATION OF THE SON

1 Why do the nations rage
and the peoples plot in vain?
2 The kings of the earth take their stand,
and the rulers conspire together
against the LORD and his Anointed One:
3 "Let's tear off their chains
and throw their ropes off of us."

4 The one enthroned in heaven laughs;
the Lord ridicules them.
5 Then he speaks to them in his anger
and terrifies them in his wrath:
6 "I have installed my king
on Zion, my holy mountain."

7 I will declare the LORD's decree.
He said to me, "You are my Son;
today I have become your Father.
8 Ask of me,
and I will make the nations your inheritance
and the ends of the earth your possession.
9 You will break them with an iron scepter;
you will shatter them like pottery."

10 So now, kings, be wise;
receive instruction, you judges of the earth.
11 Serve the LORD with reverential awe
and rejoice with trembling.
12 Pay homage to the Son or he will be angry
and you will perish in your rebellion,
for his anger may ignite at any moment.
All who take refuge in him are happy.

PSALM 3

CONFIDENCE IN TROUBLED TIMES

A psalm of David when he fled from his son Absalom.

1 LORD, how my foes increase!
There are many who attack me.
2 Many say about me,
"There is no help for him in God." *Selah*

3 But you, LORD, are a shield around me,
my glory, and the one who lifts up my head.
4 I cry aloud to the LORD,
and he answers me from his holy mountain. *Selah*

5 I lie down and sleep;
I wake again because the Lord sustains me.
6 I will not be afraid of thousands of people
who have taken their stand against me on every side.

7 Rise up, Lord!
Save me, my God!
You strike all my enemies on the cheek;
you break the teeth of the wicked.
8 Salvation belongs to the Lord;
may your blessing be on your people.   *Selah*

PSALM 16

CONFIDENCE IN THE LORD

A Miktam *of David.*

1 Protect me, God, for I take refuge in you.
2 I said to the Lord, "You are my Lord;
I have nothing good besides you."
3 As for the holy people who are in the land,
they are the noble ones.
All my delight is in them.
4 The sorrows of those who take another god
for themselves will multiply;
I will not pour out their drink offerings of blood,
and I will not speak their names with my lips.

5 Lord, you are my portion
and my cup of blessing;
you hold my future.
6 The boundary lines have fallen for me
in pleasant places;
indeed, I have a beautiful inheritance.

7 I will bless the Lord who counsels me—
even at night when my thoughts trouble me.
8 I always let the Lord guide me.
Because he is at my right hand,
I will not be shaken.

9 Therefore my heart is glad
and my whole being rejoices;
my body also rests securely.

Notes

¹⁰ For you will not abandon me to Sheol;
you will not allow your faithful one to see decay.

¹¹ You reveal the path of life to me;
in your presence is abundant joy;
at your right hand are eternal pleasures.

PSALM 17

A PRAYER FOR PROTECTION

A prayer of David.

¹ LORD, hear a just cause;
pay attention to my cry;
listen to my prayer—
from lips free of deceit.

² Let my vindication come from you,
for you see what is right.

³ You have tested my heart;
you have examined me at night.
You have tried me and found nothing evil;
I have determined that my mouth will not sin.

⁴ Concerning what people do:
by the words from your lips
I have avoided the ways of the violent.

⁵ My steps are on your paths;
my feet have not slipped.

⁶ I call on you, God,
because you will answer me;
listen closely to me; hear what I say.

⁷ Display the wonders of your faithful love,
Savior of all who seek refuge
from those who rebel against your right hand.

⁸ Protect me as the pupil of your eye;
hide me in the shadow of your wings

⁹ from the wicked who treat me violently,
my deadly enemies who surround me.

¹⁰ They are uncaring;
their mouths speak arrogantly.

¹¹ They advance against me; now they surround me.
They are determined
to throw me to the ground.

¹² They are like a lion eager to tear,
like a young lion lurking in ambush.

¹³ Rise up, LORD!
Confront him; bring him down.
With your sword, save me from the wicked.

¹⁴ With your hand, LORD, save me from men,
from men of the world
whose portion is in this life:
You fill their bellies with what you have in store;
their sons are satisfied,
and they leave their surplus to their children.

¹⁵ But I will see your face in righteousness;
when I awake, I will be satisfied with your presence.

DAILY REFLECTION QUESTIONS

1 WHAT THEMES DID YOU NOTICE IN TODAY'S PSALMS?

2 WHAT METAPHORS, IMAGERY, OR POETIC DEVICES WERE USED IN TODAY'S PSALMS TO HIGHLIGHT THESE THEMES?

Hope and Trust in God

PSALM 18

PRAISE FOR DELIVERANCE

For the choir director. Of the servant of the LORD, David, who spoke the words of this song to the LORD on the day the LORD rescued him from the grasp of all his enemies and from the power of Saul. He said:

1 I love you, LORD, my strength.
2 The LORD is my rock,
   my fortress, and my deliverer,
   my God, my rock where I seek refuge,
   my shield and the horn of my salvation,
   my stronghold.
3 I called to the LORD, who is worthy of praise,
   and I was saved from my enemies.

4 The ropes of death were wrapped around me;
   the torrents of destruction terrified me.
5 The ropes of Sheol entangled me;
   the snares of death confronted me.
6 I called to the LORD in my distress,
   and I cried to my God for help.
   From his temple he heard my voice,
   and my cry to him reached his ears.

7 Then the earth shook and quaked;
the foundations of the mountains trembled;
they shook because he burned with anger.

8 Smoke rose from his nostrils,
and consuming fire came from his mouth;
coals were set ablaze by it.

9 He bent the heavens and came down,
total darkness beneath his feet.

10 He rode on a cherub and flew,
soaring on the wings of the wind.

11 He made darkness his hiding place,
dark storm clouds his canopy around him.

12 From the radiance of his presence,
his clouds swept onward with hail and blazing coals.

13 The LORD thundered from heaven;
the Most High made his voice heard.

14 He shot his arrows and scattered them;
he hurled lightning bolts and routed them.

15 The depths of the sea became visible,
the foundations of the world were exposed,
at your rebuke, LORD,
at the blast of the breath of your nostrils.

16 He reached down from on high
and took hold of me;
he pulled me out of deep water.

17 He rescued me from my powerful enemy
and from those who hated me,
for they were too strong for me.

18 They confronted me in the day of my calamity,
but the LORD was my support.

19 He brought me out to a spacious place;
he rescued me because he delighted in me.

20 The LORD rewarded me
according to my righteousness;
he repaid me
according to the cleanness of my hands.

21 For I have kept the ways of the LORD
and have not turned from my God to wickedness.

22 Indeed, I let all his ordinances guide me
and have not disregarded his statutes.

23 I was blameless toward him
and kept myself from my iniquity.

24 So the LORD repaid me
according to my righteousness,
according to the cleanness of my hands in his sight.

25 With the faithful
you prove yourself faithful,
with the blameless
you prove yourself blameless,

26 with the pure
you prove yourself pure,
but with the crooked
you prove yourself shrewd.

27 For you rescue an oppressed people,
but you humble those with haughty eyes.

28 LORD, you light my lamp;
my God illuminates my darkness.

29 With you I can attack a barricade,
and with my God I can leap over a wall.

30 God—his way is perfect;
the word of the LORD is pure.
He is a shield to all who take refuge in him.

31 For who is God besides the LORD?
And who is a rock? Only our God.

32 God—he clothes me with strength
and makes my way perfect.

33 He makes my feet like the feet of a deer
and sets me securely on the heights.

34 He trains my hands for war;
my arms can bend a bow of bronze.

35 You have given me the shield of your salvation;
your right hand upholds me,
and your humility exalts me.

36 You make a spacious place beneath me for my steps,
and my ankles do not give way.

37 I pursue my enemies and overtake them;
I do not turn back until they are wiped out.

38 I crush them, and they cannot get up;
they fall beneath my feet.

39 You have clothed me with strength for battle;
you subdue my adversaries beneath me.

40 You have made my enemies retreat before me;
I annihilate those who hate me.

> *The LORD is my rock,*
> *my fortress, and my deliverer.*

PSALM 18:2

⁴¹ They cry for help, but there is no one to save them—
they cry to the LORD, but he does not answer them.
⁴² I pulverize them like dust before the wind;
I trample them like mud in the streets.

⁴³ You have freed me from the feuds among the people;
you have appointed me the head of nations;
a people I had not known serve me.
⁴⁴ Foreigners submit to me cringing;
as soon as they hear they obey me.
⁴⁵ Foreigners lose heart
and come trembling from their fortifications.

⁴⁶ The LORD lives—blessed be my rock!
The God of my salvation is exalted.
⁴⁷ God—he grants me vengeance
and subdues peoples under me.
⁴⁸ He frees me from my enemies.
You exalt me above my adversaries;
you rescue me from violent men.
⁴⁹ Therefore I will give thanks to you among the
nations, LORD;
I will sing praises about your name.
⁵⁰ He gives great victories to his king;
he shows loyalty to his anointed,
to David and his descendants forever.

PSALM 22

FROM SUFFERING TO PRAISE

For the choir director: according to "The Deer of the Dawn."
A psalm of David.

¹ My God, my God, why have you abandoned me?
Why are you so far from my deliverance
and from my words of groaning?
² My God, I cry by day, but you do not answer,
by night, yet I have no rest.
³ But you are holy,
enthroned on the praises of Israel.
⁴ Our ancestors trusted in you;
they trusted, and you rescued them.
⁵ They cried to you and were set free;
they trusted in you and were not disgraced.

⁶ But I am a worm and not a man,
scorned by mankind and despised by people.
⁷ Everyone who sees me mocks me;
they sneer and shake their heads:
⁸ "He relies on the LORD;
let him save him;
let the LORD rescue him,
since he takes pleasure in him."

⁹ It was you who brought me out of the womb,
making me secure at my mother's breast.
¹⁰ I was given over to you at birth;
you have been my God from my mother's womb.

11   Don't be far from me, because distress is near
and there's no one to help.

12   Many bulls surround me;
strong ones of Bashan encircle me.
13   They open their mouths against me—
lions, mauling and roaring.
14   I am poured out like water,
and all my bones are disjointed;
my heart is like wax,
melting within me.
15   My strength is dried up like baked clay;
my tongue sticks to the roof of my mouth.
You put me into the dust of death.
16   For dogs have surrounded me;
a gang of evildoers has closed in on me;
they pierced my hands and my feet.
17   I can count all my bones;
people look and stare at me.
18   They divided my garments among themselves,
and they cast lots for my clothing.

19   But you, LORD, don't be far away.
My strength, come quickly to help me.
20   Rescue my life from the sword,
my only life from the power of these dogs.
21   Save me from the lion's mouth,
from the horns of wild oxen.
You answered me!
22   I will proclaim your name to my brothers and sisters;
I will praise you in the assembly.
23   You who fear the LORD, praise him!
All you descendants of Jacob, honor him!
All you descendants of Israel, revere him!
24   For he has not despised or abhorred
the torment of the oppressed.
He did not hide his face from him
but listened when he cried to him for help.

25   I will give praise in the great assembly
because of you;
I will fulfill my vows
before those who fear you.

26   The humble will eat and be satisfied;
      those who seek the Lord will praise him.
      May your hearts live forever!

27   All the ends of the earth will remember
      and turn to the Lord.
      All the families of the nations
      will bow down before you,
28   for kingship belongs to the Lord;
      he rules the nations.
29   All who prosper on earth will eat and bow down;
      all those who go down to the dust
      will kneel before him—
      even the one who cannot preserve his life.
30   Their descendants will serve him;
      the next generation will be told about the Lord.
31   They will come and declare his righteousness;
      to a people yet to be born
      they will declare what he has done.

PSALM 23

THE GOOD SHEPHERD

A psalm of David.

1   The Lord is my shepherd;
      I have what I need.
2   He lets me lie down in green pastures;
      he leads me beside quiet waters.
3   He renews my life;
      he leads me along the right paths
      for his name's sake.
4   Even when I go through the darkest valley,
      I fear no danger,
      for you are with me;
      your rod and your staff—they comfort me.

5   You prepare a table before me
      in the presence of my enemies;
      you anoint my head with oil;
      my cup overflows.
6   Only goodness and faithful love will pursue me
      all the days of my life,
      and I will dwell in the house of the Lord
      as long as I live.

DAILY REFLECTION QUESTIONS

1

WHAT THEMES DID YOU NOTICE IN TODAY'S PSALMS?

2

WHAT METAPHORS, IMAGERY, OR POETIC DEVICES WERE
USED IN TODAY'S PSALMS TO HIGHLIGHT THESE THEMES?

Remember God's

(I)

Faithfulness

PSALM 27

MY STRONGHOLD

Of David.

1 The Lord is my light and my salvation—
 whom should I fear?
 The Lord is the stronghold of my life—
 whom should I dread?
2 When evildoers came against me to devour my flesh,
 my foes and my enemies stumbled and fell.
3 Though an army deploys against me,
 my heart will not be afraid;
 though a war breaks out against me,
 I will still be confident.

4 I have asked one thing from the Lord;
 it is what I desire:
 to dwell in the house of the Lord
 all the days of my life,
 gazing on the beauty of the Lord
 and seeking him in his temple.
5 For he will conceal me in his shelter
 in the day of adversity;
 he will hide me under the cover of his tent;
 he will set me high on a rock.
6 Then my head will be high
 above my enemies around me;
 I will offer sacrifices in his tent with shouts of joy.
 I will sing and make music to the Lord.

7 Lord, hear my voice when I call;
 be gracious to me and answer me.
8 My heart says this about you:
 "Seek his face."
 Lord, I will seek your face.
9 Do not hide your face from me;
 do not turn your servant away in anger.
 You have been my helper;
 do not leave me or abandon me,
 God of my salvation.
10 Even if my father and mother abandon me,
 the Lord cares for me.

11 Because of my adversaries,
 show me your way, Lord,
 and lead me on a level path.
12 Do not give me over to the will of my foes,
 for false witnesses rise up against me,
 breathing violence.

13 I am certain that I will see the Lord's goodness
 in the land of the living.
14 Wait for the Lord;
 be strong, and let your heart be courageous.
 Wait for the Lord.

PSALM 30

JOY IN THE MORNING

A psalm; a dedication song for the house. Of David.

1 I will exalt you, Lord,
 because you have lifted me up
 and have not allowed my enemies
 to triumph over me.
2 Lord my God,
 I cried to you for help, and you healed me.
3 Lord, you brought me up from Sheol;
 you spared me from among those
 going down to the Pit.

4 Sing to the Lord, you his faithful ones,
 and praise his holy name.
5 For his anger lasts only a moment,
 but his favor, a lifetime.
 Weeping may stay overnight,
 but there is joy in the morning.

6 When I was secure, I said,
 "I will never be shaken."
7 Lord, when you showed your favor,
 you made me stand like a strong mountain;
 when you hid your face, I was terrified.

8 Lord, I called to you;
  I sought favor from my Lord:
9 "What gain is there in my death,
  if I go down to the Pit?
  Will the dust praise you?
  Will it proclaim your truth?
10 Lord, listen and be gracious to me;
  Lord, be my helper."

11 You turned my lament into dancing;
  you removed my sackcloth
  and clothed me with gladness,
12 so that I can sing to you and not be silent.
  Lord my God, I will praise you forever.

PSALMS
40–41

————

Book I ends with
David's personal
lament and
declaration of
trust in God.

PSALM 40

THANKSGIVING AND A CRY FOR HELP

For the choir director. A psalm of David.

1 I waited patiently for the Lord,
  and he turned to me and heard my cry for help.
2 He brought me up from a desolate pit,
  out of the muddy clay,
  and set my feet on a rock,
  making my steps secure.
3 He put a new song in my mouth,
  a hymn of praise to our God.
  Many will see and fear,
  and they will trust in the Lord.

4 How happy is anyone
  who has put his trust in the Lord
  and has not turned to the proud
  or to those who run after lies!
5 Lord my God, you have done many things—
  your wondrous works and your plans for us;
  none can compare with you.
  If I were to report and speak of them,
  they are more than can be told.

6 You do not delight in sacrifice and offering;
  you open my ears to listen.
  You do not ask for a whole burnt offering or a sin offering.

7   Then I said, "See, I have come;
    in the scroll it is written about me.
8   I delight to do your will, my God,
    and your instruction is deep within me."

9   I proclaim righteousness in the great assembly;
    see, I do not keep my mouth closed—
    as you know, LORD.
10 I did not hide your righteousness in my heart;
    I spoke about your faithfulness and salvation;
    I did not conceal your constant love and truth
    from the great assembly.

11 LORD, you do not withhold your compassion from me.
    Your constant love and truth will always guard me.
12 For troubles without number have surrounded me;
    my iniquities have overtaken me; I am unable to see.
    They are more than the hairs of my head,
    and my courage leaves me.
13 LORD, be pleased to rescue me;
    hurry to help me, LORD.

14 Let those who intend to take my life
    be disgraced and confounded.
    Let those who wish me harm
    be turned back and humiliated.
15 Let those who say to me, "Aha, aha!"
    be appalled because of their shame.

16 Let all who seek you rejoice and be glad in you;
    let those who love your salvation continually say,
    "The LORD is great!"
17 I am oppressed and needy;
    may the Lord think of me.
    You are my helper and my deliverer;
    my God, do not delay.

PSALM 41

VICTORY IN SPITE OF BETRAYAL

For the choir director. A psalm of David.

1   Happy is one who is considerate of the poor;
    the LORD will save him in a day of adversity.

Notes

2   The LORD will keep him and preserve him;
     he will be blessed in the land.
     You will not give him over to the desire of his enemies.
3   The LORD will sustain him on his sickbed;
     you will heal him on the bed where he lies.

4   I said, "LORD, be gracious to me;
     heal me, for I have sinned against you."
5   My enemies speak maliciously about me:
     "When will he die and be forgotten?"
6   When one of them comes to visit, he speaks deceitfully;
     he stores up evil in his heart;
     he goes out and talks.
7   All who hate me whisper together about me;
     they plan to harm me.
8   "Something awful has overwhelmed him,
     and he won't rise again from where he lies!"
9   Even my friend in whom I trusted,
     one who ate my bread,
     has raised his heel against me.

10   But you, LORD, be gracious to me and raise me up;
     then I will repay them.
11   By this I know that you delight in me:
     my enemy does not shout in triumph over me.
12   You supported me because of my integrity
     and set me in your presence forever.

13   Blessed be the LORD God of Israel,
     from everlasting to everlasting.
     Amen and amen.

DAILY REFLECTION QUESTIONS

1

WHAT THEMES DID YOU NOTICE IN TODAY'S PSALMS?

2

WHAT METAPHORS, IMAGERY, OR POETIC DEVICES WERE
USED IN TODAY'S PSALMS TO HIGHLIGHT THESE THEMES?

BOOK

I

Response

1

LOOK BACK AT YOUR DAILY REFLECTIONS. HOW DO EACH OF THE THEMES YOU NOTED CONTRIBUTE TO THE OVERALL MESSAGE OF BOOK I?

LOOK BACK AT PAGE 23 IF YOU NEED A REMINDER.

2

HOW DO THESE THEMES ANTICIPATE JESUS, THE ETERNAL KING?

3

HOW IS GOD DESCRIBED IN BOOK I?

4

WHAT DO THE PSALMS IN BOOK I MODEL FOR YOU AS A WORSHIPER?

BOOK

II

Psalms 42–72

INTRODUCTION

Like Book I, the collection of psalms in Book II express lament and distress about present circumstances and conditions while still looking to the faithfulness of God. These psalms act as a reminder that His glory, goodness, and power are worthy of celebration in Israel and among the nations.

While the psalms in Book I are almost exclusively attributed to David, Book II's authors include temple keepers and singers who served under David and his son, King Solomon. Book II closes with a coronation prayer for David's line to lead Israel in righteousness and truth.

KEY FACTS

1   Many psalms in this section were attributed to Asaph and the Sons of Korah. This group of Levitical priests descended from Korah served as gatekeepers and temple singers (1Ch 9:17–21; 2Ch 20:14–19).

2   These psalms primarily use the name *Elohim*, the name translated "God" in most English Bibles. This general name demonstrates His unmatched power and majesty.

3   This book contains many psalms known as "historical psalms" that are connected to specific events in David's life.

DAY 4

Longing for God's Justice

PSALMS 42–44

———

Book II opens with prayers for God's presence and justice in the midst of distress.

PSALM 42

LONGING FOR GOD

For the choir director. A Maskil *of the sons of Korah.*

1 As a deer longs for flowing streams,
so I long for you, God.
2 I thirst for God, the living God.
When can I come and appear before God?
3 My tears have been my food day and night,
while all day long people say to me,
"Where is your God?"
4 I remember this as I pour out my heart:
how I walked with many,
leading the festive procession to the house of God,
with joyful and thankful shouts.

5 Why, my soul, are you so dejected?
Why are you in such turmoil?
Put your hope in God, for I will still praise him,
my Savior and my God.
6 I am deeply depressed;
therefore I remember you from the land of Jordan
and the peaks of Hermon, from Mount Mizar.
7 Deep calls to deep in the roar of your waterfalls;
all your breakers and your billows have swept over me.
8 The LORD will send his faithful love by day;
his song will be with me in the night—
a prayer to the God of my life.

9   I will say to God, my rock,
"Why have you forgotten me?
Why must I go about in sorrow
because of the enemy's oppression?"

10   My adversaries taunt me,
as if crushing my bones,
while all day long they say to me,
"Where is your God?"

11   Why, my soul, are you so dejected?
Why are you in such turmoil?
Put your hope in God, for I will still praise him,
my Savior and my God.

PSALM 43

1   Vindicate me, God, and champion my cause
against an unfaithful nation;
rescue me from the deceitful and unjust person.

2   For you are the God of my refuge.
Why have you rejected me?
Why must I go about in sorrow
because of the enemy's oppression?

3   Send your light and your truth; let them lead me.
Let them bring me to your holy mountain,
to your dwelling place.

4   Then I will come to the altar of God,
to God, my greatest joy.
I will praise you with the lyre,
God, my God.

5   Why, my soul, are you so dejected?
Why are you in such turmoil?
Put your hope in God, for I will still praise him,
my Savior and my God.

PSALM 44

ISRAEL'S COMPLAINT

For the choir director. A Maskil *of the sons of Korah.*

1   God, we have heard with our ears—
our ancestors have told us—
the work you accomplished in their days,
in days long ago:

As a deer longs for flowing streams,
so I long for you, God.

PSALM 42:1

2   In order to plant them,
     you displaced the nations by your hand;
     in order to settle them,
     you brought disaster on the peoples.
3   For they did not take the land by their sword—
     their arm did not bring them victory—
     but by your right hand, your arm,
     and the light of your face,
     because you were favorable toward them.

4   You are my King, my God,
     who ordains victories for Jacob.
5   Through you we drive back our foes;
     through your name we trample our enemies.
6   For I do not trust in my bow,
     and my sword does not bring me victory.
7   But you give us victory over our foes
     and let those who hate us be disgraced.
8   We boast in God all day long;
     we will praise your name forever.   *Selah*

9   But you have rejected and humiliated us;
     you do not march out with our armies.
10   You make us retreat from the foe,
     and those who hate us
     have taken plunder for themselves.
11   You hand us over to be eaten like sheep
     and scatter us among the nations.
12   You sell your people for nothing;
     you make no profit from selling them.
13   You make us an object of reproach to our neighbors,
     a source of mockery and ridicule to those around us.

14   You make us a joke among the nations,
     a laughingstock among the peoples.
15   My disgrace is before me all day long,
     and shame has covered my face,
16   because of the taunts of the scorner and reviler,
     because of the enemy and avenger.

17   All this has happened to us,
     but we have not forgotten you
     or betrayed your covenant.
18   Our hearts have not turned back;
     our steps have not strayed from your path.
19   But you have crushed us in a haunt of jackals
     and have covered us with deepest darkness.
20   If we had forgotten the name of our God
     and spread out our hands to a foreign god,
21   wouldn't God have found this out,
     since he knows the secrets of the heart?
22   Because of you we are being put to death all day long;
     we are counted as sheep to be slaughtered.

23   Wake up, LORD! Why are you sleeping?
     Get up! Don't reject us forever!
24   Why do you hide
     and forget our affliction and oppression?
25   For we have sunk down to the dust;
     our bodies cling to the ground.
26   Rise up! Help us!
     Redeem us because of your faithful love.

DAILY REFLECTION QUESTIONS

II

1

WHAT THEMES DID YOU NOTICE IN TODAY'S PSALMS?

2

WHAT METAPHORS, IMAGERY, OR POETIC DEVICES WERE
USED IN TODAY'S PSALMS TO HIGHLIGHT THESE THEMES?

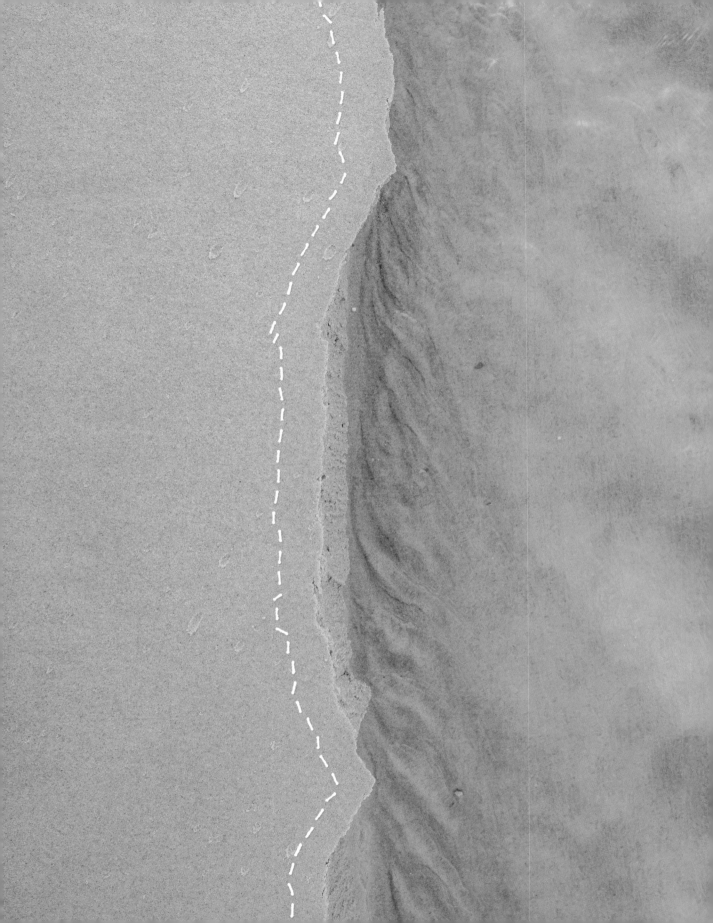

II

Seek God's Deliverance

PSALM 51

A PRAYER FOR RESTORATION

*For the choir director. A psalm of David, when the prophet
Nathan came to him after he had gone to Bathsheba.*

1   Be gracious to me, God,
    according to your faithful love;
    according to your abundant compassion,
    blot out my rebellion.
2   Completely wash away my guilt
    and cleanse me from my sin.
3   For I am conscious of my rebellion,
    and my sin is always before me.
4   Against you—you alone—I have sinned
    and done this evil in your sight.
    So you are right when you pass sentence;
    you are blameless when you judge.
5   Indeed, I was guilty when I was born;
    I was sinful when my mother conceived me.

6   Surely you desire integrity in the inner self,
    and you teach me wisdom deep within.
7   Purify me with hyssop, and I will be clean;
    wash me, and I will be whiter than snow.

8   Let me hear joy and gladness;
    let the bones you have crushed rejoice.
9   Turn your face away from my sins
    and blot out all my guilt.

10 God, create a clean heart for me
    and renew a steadfast spirit within me.
11 Do not banish me from your presence
    or take your Holy Spirit from me.
12 Restore the joy of your salvation to me,
    and sustain me by giving me a willing spirit.
13 Then I will teach the rebellious your ways,
    and sinners will return to you.

14 Save me from the guilt of bloodshed, God—
    God of my salvation—
    and my tongue will sing of your righteousness.
15 Lord, open my lips,
    and my mouth will declare your praise.

I will seek refuge in the shadow of
your wings until danger passes.

PSALM 57:1

16 You do not want a sacrifice, or I would give it;
you are not pleased with a burnt offering.
17 The sacrifice pleasing to God is a broken spirit.
You will not despise a broken and humbled
heart, God.

18 In your good pleasure, cause Zion to prosper;
build the walls of Jerusalem.
19 Then you will delight in righteous sacrifices,
whole burnt offerings;
then bulls will be offered on your altar.

PSALM 56

A CALL FOR GOD'S PROTECTION

For the choir director: according to "A Silent Dove Far Away."
A Miktam of David. When the Philistines seized him in Gath.

1 Be gracious to me, God, for a man is trampling me;
he fights and oppresses me all day long.
2 My adversaries trample me all day,
for many arrogantly fight against me.

3 When I am afraid,
I will trust in you.
4 In God, whose word I praise,
in God I trust; I will not be afraid.
What can mere mortals do to me?

5 They twist my words all day long;
all their thoughts against me are evil.
6 They stir up strife, they lurk,

they watch my steps
while they wait to take my life.
7 Will they escape in spite of such sin?
God, bring down the nations in wrath.

8 You yourself have recorded my wanderings.
Put my tears in your bottle.
Are they not in your book?
9 Then my enemies will retreat on the day when I call.
This I know: God is for me.

10 In God, whose word I praise,
in the LORD, whose word I praise,
11 in God I trust; I will not be afraid.
What can mere humans do to me?

12 I am obligated by vows to you, God;
I will make my thanksgiving sacrifices to you.
13 For you rescued me from death,
even my feet from stumbling,
to walk before God in the light of life.

PSALM 57

PRAISE FOR GOD'S PROTECTION

For the choir director: "Do Not Destroy." A Miktam of David.
When he fled before Saul into the cave.

1 Be gracious to me, God, be gracious to me,
for I take refuge in you.
I will seek refuge in the shadow of your wings
until danger passes.

2 I call to God Most High,
to God who fulfills his purpose for me.
3 He reaches down from heaven and saves me,
challenging the one who tramples me.   *Selah*
God sends his faithful love and truth.
4 I am surrounded by lions;
I lie down among devouring lions—
people whose teeth are spears and arrows,
whose tongues are sharp swords.
5 God, be exalted above the heavens;
let your glory be over the whole earth.
6 They prepared a net for my steps;
I was despondent.
They dug a pit ahead of me,
but they fell into it!   *Selah*

7 My heart is confident, God, my heart is confident.
I will sing; I will sing praises.
8 Wake up, my soul!
Wake up, harp and lyre!
I will wake up the dawn.
9 I will praise you, Lord, among the peoples;
I will sing praises to you among the nations.
10 For your faithful love is as high as the heavens;
your faithfulness reaches the clouds.
11 God, be exalted above the heavens;
let your glory be over the whole earth.

PSALM 59

GOD OUR STRONGHOLD

For the choir director: "Do Not Destroy." A Miktam *of David.
When Saul sent agents to watch the house and kill him.*

1 Rescue me from my enemies, my God;
protect me from those who rise up against me.
2 Rescue me from evildoers,
and save me from men of bloodshed.
3 Because look, Lord, they set an ambush for me.
Powerful men attack me,
but not because of any sin or rebellion of mine.
4 For no fault of mine,
they run and take up a position.
Awake to help me, and take notice.

Notes

5   Lord God of Armies, you are the God of Israel.
    Rise up to punish all the nations;
    do not show favor to any wicked traitors.   *Selah*

6   They return at evening, snarling like dogs
    and prowling around the city.
7   Look, they spew from their mouths—
    sharp words from their lips.
    "For who," they say, "will hear?"
8   But you laugh at them, Lord;
    you ridicule all the nations.
9   I will keep watch for you, my strength,
    because God is my stronghold.
10 My faithful God will come to meet me;
    God will let me look down on my adversaries.

11 Do not kill them; otherwise, my people will forget.
    By your power, make them homeless wanderers
    and bring them down,
    Lord, our shield.
12 For the sin of their mouths and the words of their lips,
    let them be caught in their pride.
    They utter curses and lies.
13 Consume them in fury;
    consume them until they are gone.
    Then people will know throughout the earth
    that God rules over Jacob.   *Selah*

14 And they return at evening, snarling like dogs
    and prowling around the city.
15 They scavenge for food;
    they growl if they are not satisfied.

16 But I will sing of your strength
    and will joyfully proclaim
    your faithful love in the morning.
    For you have been a stronghold for me,
    a refuge in my day of trouble.
17 To you, my strength, I sing praises,
    because God is my stronghold—
    my faithful God.

PSALM 64

PROTECTION FROM EVILDOERS

For the choir director. A psalm of David.

1   God, hear my voice when I am in anguish.
    Protect my life from the terror of the enemy.
2   Hide me from the scheming of wicked people,
    from the mob of evildoers,
3   who sharpen their tongues like swords
    and aim bitter words like arrows,
4   shooting from concealed places at the blameless.
    They shoot at him suddenly and are not afraid.
5   They adopt an evil plan;
    they talk about hiding traps and say,
    "Who will see them?"
6   They devise crimes and say,
    "We have perfected a secret plan."
    The inner man and the heart are mysterious.

7   But God will shoot them with arrows;
    suddenly, they will be wounded.
8   They will be made to stumble;
    their own tongues work against them.
    All who see them will shake their heads.
9   Then everyone will fear
    and will tell about God's work,
    for they will understand what he has done.

10 The righteous one rejoices in the Lord
    and takes refuge in him;
    all those who are upright in heart
    will offer praise.

II

1

WHAT THEMES DID YOU NOTICE IN TODAY'S PSALMS?

2

WHAT METAPHORS, IMAGERY, OR POETIC DEVICES WERE
USED IN TODAY'S PSALMS TO HIGHLIGHT THESE THEMES?

Grace Day

·——·——·——·——·——·——·——·——·——·

Take this day to catch up on your reading, pray,
and rest in the presence of the Lord.

*"I am the good shepherd.
The good shepherd lays down
his life for the sheep."*

JOHN 10:11

Weekly
Truth

wwwwwwwwwwwwwwwwwwwwwwwwwwwwwwwwwwwwwwwwwwwwwwwwww

Scripture is God-breathed and true. When we memorize it, we carry His Word with us wherever we go.

The key passage for this reading plan is Psalm 40:1–3. Throughout the remainder of this reading plan, we will memorize verse 3, David's song of thanksgiving for God's deliverance. We will start with the first two lines. Since the psalms were meant to be sung, try adding a tune of your own as you commit this verse to memory.

AMEN AND AMEN: A JOURNEY THROUGH THE PSALMS

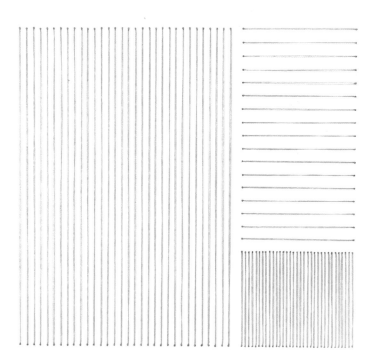

**HE PUT A NEW SONG IN MY MOUTH,
A HYMN OF PRAISE TO OUR GOD.**
MANY WILL SEE AND FEAR,
AND THEY WILL TRUST IN THE LORD.

PSALM 40:3

See tips for memorizing Scripture on page 144.

Praise God Alone

PSALM 66

PRAISE FOR GOD'S MIGHTY ACTS

For the choir director. A song. A psalm.

1   Let the whole earth shout joyfully to God!
2   Sing about the glory of his name;
    make his praise glorious.
3   Say to God, "How awe-inspiring are your works!
    Your enemies will cringe before you
    because of your great strength.
4   The whole earth will worship you
    and sing praise to you.
    They will sing praise to your name."   *Selah*

5   Come and see the wonders of God;
    his acts for humanity are awe-inspiring.
6   He turned the sea into dry land,
    and they crossed the river on foot.
    There we rejoiced in him.
7   He rules forever by his might;
    he keeps his eye on the nations.
    The rebellious should not exalt themselves.   *Selah*
8   Bless our God, you peoples;
    let the sound of his praise be heard.

Let the peoples praise you,
God; let all the peoples praise you.

PSALM 67:3

9   He keeps us alive
    and does not allow our feet to slip.

10 For you, God, tested us;
    you refined us as silver is refined.

11 You lured us into a trap;
    you placed burdens on our backs.

12 You let men ride over our heads;
    we went through fire and water,
    but you brought us out to abundance.

13 I will enter your house with burnt offerings;
    I will pay you my vows

14 that my lips promised
    and my mouth spoke during my distress.

15 I will offer you fattened sheep as burnt offerings,
    with the fragrant smoke of rams;
    I will sacrifice bulls with goats.   *Selah*

16 Come and listen, all who fear God,
    and I will tell what he has done for me.

17 I cried out to him with my mouth,
    and praise was on my tongue.

18 If I had been aware of malice in my heart,
    the Lord would not have listened.

19 However, God has listened;
    he has paid attention to the sound of my prayer.

20 Blessed be God!
    He has not turned away my prayer
    or turned his faithful love from me.

PSALM 67

ALL WILL PRAISE GOD

For the choir director: with stringed instruments. A psalm.
A song.

1   May God be gracious to us and bless us;
    may he make his face shine upon us   *Selah*

2   so that your way may be known on earth,
    your salvation among all nations.

3   Let the peoples praise you, God;
    let all the peoples praise you.

4   Let the nations rejoice and shout for joy,
    for you judge the peoples with fairness
    and lead the nations on earth.   *Selah*

5   Let the peoples praise you, God,
    let all the peoples praise you.

6   The earth has produced its harvest;
    God, our God, blesses us.

7   God will bless us,
    and all the ends of the earth will fear him.

PSALM 68

GOD'S MAJESTIC POWER

For the choir director. A psalm of David. A song.

1   God arises. His enemies scatter,
    and those who hate him flee from his presence.

2   As smoke is blown away,
    so you blow them away.
    As wax melts before the fire,
    so the wicked are destroyed before God.
3   But the righteous are glad;
    they rejoice before God and celebrate with joy.

4   Sing to God! Sing praises to his name.
    Exalt him who rides on the clouds—
    his name is the LORD—and celebrate before him.
5   God in his holy dwelling is
    a father of the fatherless
    and a champion of widows.
6   God provides homes for those who are deserted.
    He leads out the prisoners to prosperity,
    but the rebellious live in a scorched land.

7   God, when you went out before your people,
    when you marched through the desert,   *Selah*
8   the earth trembled and the skies poured rain
    before God, the God of Sinai,
    before God, the God of Israel.
9   You, God, showered abundant rain;
    you revived your inheritance when it languished.
10 Your people settled in it;
    God, you provided for the poor by your goodness.

11 The Lord gave the command;
    a great company of women brought the good news:
12 "The kings of the armies flee—they flee!"
    She who stays at home divides the spoil.
13 While you lie among the sheep pens,
    the wings of a dove are covered with silver,
    and its feathers with glistening gold.
14 When the Almighty scattered kings in the land,
    it snowed on Zalmon.

15 Mount Bashan is God's towering mountain;
    Mount Bashan is a mountain of many peaks.
16 Why gaze with envy, you mountain peaks,
    at the mountain God desired for his abode?
    The LORD will dwell there forever!

17 God's chariots are tens of thousands,
  thousands and thousands;
  the Lord is among them in the sanctuary
  as he was at Sinai.
18 You ascended to the heights, taking away captives;
  you received gifts from people,
  even from the rebellious,
  so that the LORD God might dwell there.

19 Blessed be the Lord!
  Day after day he bears our burdens;
  God is our salvation.   *Selah*
20 Our God is a God of salvation,
  and escape from death belongs to the LORD my Lord.
21 Surely God crushes the heads of his enemies,
  the hairy brow of one who goes on in his guilty acts.
22 The Lord said, "I will bring them back from Bashan;
  I will bring them back from the depths of the sea
23 so that your foot may wade in blood
  and your dogs' tongues may have their share
  from the enemies."
24 People have seen your procession, God,
  the procession of my God,
  my King, in the sanctuary.
25 Singers lead the way,
  with musicians following;
  among them are young women
  playing tambourines.
26 Bless God in the assemblies;
  bless the LORD from the fountain of Israel.
27 There is Benjamin, the youngest, leading them,
  the rulers of Judah in their assembly,
  the rulers of Zebulun, the rulers of Naphtali.

28 Your God has decreed your strength.
  Show your strength, God,
  you who have acted on our behalf.
29 Because of your temple at Jerusalem,
  kings will bring tribute to you.
30 Rebuke the beast in the reeds,
  the herd of bulls with the calves of the peoples.
  Trample underfoot those with bars of silver.
  Scatter the peoples who take pleasure in war.

31 Ambassadors will come from Egypt;
  Cush will stretch out its hands to God.

32 Sing to God, you kingdoms of the earth;
  sing praise to the Lord,   *Selah*
33 to him who rides in the ancient, highest heavens.
  Look, he thunders with his powerful voice!
34 Ascribe power to God.
  His majesty is over Israel;
  his power is among the clouds.
35 God, you are awe-inspiring in your sanctuaries.
  The God of Israel gives power and strength to
    his people.
  Blessed be God!

DAILY REFLECTION QUESTIONS

1   WHAT THEMES DID YOU NOTICE IN TODAY'S PSALMS?

2   WHAT METAPHORS, IMAGERY, OR POETIC DEVICES WERE
     USED IN TODAY'S PSALMS TO HIGHLIGHT THESE THEMES?

Prayers for

(II)

DAY 9

God's Blessing

PSALM 71

GOD'S HELP IN OLD AGE

Book II ends with
David's prayers
reflecting on the
transition of power.

1   Lord, I seek refuge in you;
let me never be disgraced.

2   In your justice, rescue and deliver me;
listen closely to me and save me.

3   Be a rock of refuge for me,
where I can always go.
Give the command to save me,
for you are my rock and fortress.

4   Deliver me, my God, from the power of the wicked,
from the grasp of the unjust and oppressive.

5   For you are my hope, Lord God,
my confidence from my youth.

6   I have leaned on you from birth;
you took me from my mother's womb.
My praise is always about you.

7   I am like a miraculous sign to many,
and you are my strong refuge.

8   My mouth is full of praise
and honor to you all day long.

9   Don't discard me in my old age.
As my strength fails, do not abandon me.

10   For my enemies talk about me,
and those who spy on me plot together,

11   saying, "God has abandoned him;
chase him and catch him,
for there is no one to rescue him."

12   God, do not be far from me;
my God, hurry to help me.

13   May my adversaries be disgraced and destroyed;
may those who intend to harm me
be covered with disgrace and humiliation.

14   But I will hope continually
and will praise you more and more.

15   My mouth will tell about your righteousness
and your salvation all day long,
though I cannot sum them up.

16   I come because of the mighty acts of the Lord God;
I will proclaim your righteousness, yours alone.

17   God, you have taught me from my youth,
and I still proclaim your wondrous works.

18 Even while I am old and gray,
God, do not abandon me,
while I proclaim your power
to another generation,
your strength to all who are to come.

19 Your righteousness reaches the heights, God,
you who have done great things;
God, who is like you?

20 You caused me to experience
many troubles and misfortunes,
but you will revive me again.
You will bring me up again,
even from the depths of the earth.

21 You will increase my honor
and comfort me once again.

22 Therefore, I will praise you with a harp
for your faithfulness, my God;
I will sing to you with a lyre,
Holy One of Israel.

23 My lips will shout for joy
when I sing praise to you
because you have redeemed me.

24 Therefore, my tongue will proclaim
your righteousness all day long,
for those who intend to harm me
will be disgraced and confounded.

PSALM 72

A PRAYER FOR THE KING

Of Solomon.

1 God, give your justice to the king
and your righteousness to the king's son.

2 He will judge your people with righteousness
and your afflicted ones with justice.

3 May the mountains bring well-being to the people
and the hills, righteousness.

4 May he vindicate the afflicted among the people,
help the poor,
and crush the oppressor.

5 May they fear you while the sun endures
and as long as the moon, throughout all generations.

6 May the king be like rain that falls on the cut grass,
like spring showers that water the earth.

7 May the righteous flourish in his days
and well-being abound
until the moon is no more.

8 May he rule from sea to sea
and from the Euphrates
to the ends of the earth.

9 May desert tribes kneel before him
and his enemies lick the dust.

10 May the kings of Tarshish
and the coasts and islands bring tribute,
the kings of Sheba and Seba offer gifts.

11 Let all kings bow in homage to him,
all nations serve him.

12 For he will rescue the poor who cry out
and the afflicted who have no helper.

13 He will have pity on the poor and helpless
and save the lives of the poor.

14 He will redeem them from oppression and violence,
for their lives are precious in his sight.

15 May he live long!
May gold from Sheba be given to him.
May prayer be offered for him continually,
and may he be blessed all day long.

16 May there be plenty of grain in the land;
may it wave on the tops of the mountains.
May its crops be like Lebanon.
May people flourish in the cities
like the grass of the field.

17 May his name endure forever;
as long as the sun shines,
may his fame increase.
May all nations be blessed by him
and call him blessed.

18 Blessed be the LORD God, the God of Israel,
who alone does wonders.

19 Blessed be his glorious name forever;
the whole earth is filled with his glory.
Amen and amen.

20 The prayers of David son of Jesse are concluded.

DAILY REFLECTION QUESTIONS

1

WHAT THEMES DID YOU NOTICE IN TODAY'S PSALMS?

2

WHAT METAPHORS, IMAGERY, OR POETIC DEVICES WERE
USED IN TODAY'S PSALMS TO HIGHLIGHT THESE THEMES?

BOOK

II

Response

1

LOOK BACK AT YOUR DAILY REFLECTIONS. HOW DO EACH OF THE THEMES YOU NOTED CONTRIBUTE TO THE OVERALL MESSAGE OF BOOK II?

LOOK BACK AT PAGE 45 IF YOU NEED A REMINDER.

2

HOW DO THESE THEMES ANTICIPATE JESUS, THE ETERNAL KING?

3

HOW IS GOD DESCRIBED IN BOOK II?

4

WHAT DO THE PSALMS IN BOOK II MODEL FOR YOU AS A WORSHIPER?

BOOK

III

Psalms 73–89

INTRODUCTION

While Book II ends on a high note with the anticipation of a righteous monarchy, the overall somber tone of Book III reflects the downward spiritual slope of David's descendants and Israel. Though Book III contains threads of hope, it is often labeled as the "dark" book of the Psalter because of its focus on lament. Book III is also unique in describing Israel's spiritual and physical circumstances from God's perspective. It ends with despair and confusion over God's seemingly unfulfilled promises regarding the throne of David.

KEY FACTS

1   Many of these psalms are attributed to Asaph and
     were meant for liturgical worship in the temple.

2   A BRIEF HISTORY OF ISRAEL

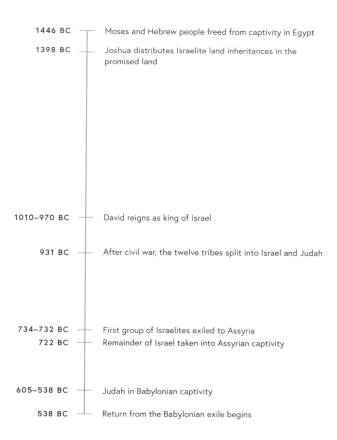

1446 BC ——— Moses and Hebrew people freed from captivity in Egypt

1398 BC ——— Joshua distributes Israelite land inheritances in the
             promised land

1010–970 BC ——— David reigns as king of Israel

931 BC ——— After civil war, the twelve tribes split into Israel and Judah

734–732 BC ——— First group of Israelites exiled to Assyria
722 BC ——— Remainder of Israel taken into Assyrian captivity

605–538 BC ——— Judah in Babylonian captivity

538 BC ——— Return from the Babylonian exile begins

Asking God to Remember

PSALMS
73–74

Book III opens with
expressions of
doubt, confusion,
and confidence in
God's deliverance.

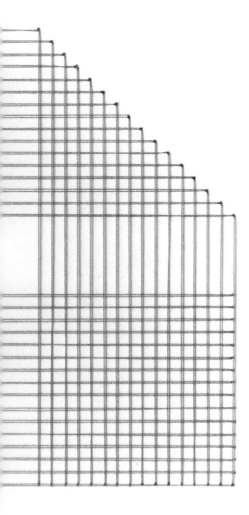

PSALM 73

GOD'S WAYS VINDICATED

A psalm of Asaph.

1   God is indeed good to Israel,
     to the pure in heart.
2   But as for me, my feet almost slipped;
     my steps nearly went astray.
3   For I envied the arrogant;
     I saw the prosperity of the wicked.

4   They have an easy time until they die,
     and their bodies are well fed.
5   They are not in trouble like others;
     they are not afflicted like most people.
6   Therefore, pride is their necklace,
     and violence covers them like a garment.
7   Their eyes bulge out from fatness;
     the imaginations of their hearts run wild.
8   They mock, and they speak maliciously;
     they arrogantly threaten oppression.
9   They set their mouths against heaven,
     and their tongues strut across the earth.
10   Therefore his people turn to them
     and drink in their overflowing words.
11   The wicked say, "How can God know?
     Does the Most High know everything?"
12   Look at them—the wicked!
     They are always at ease,
     and they increase their wealth.

13   Did I purify my heart
       and wash my hands in innocence for nothing?

14   For I am afflicted all day long
       and punished every morning.

15   If I had decided to say these things aloud,
       I would have betrayed your people.

16   When I tried to understand all this,
       it seemed hopeless

17   until I entered God's sanctuary.
       Then I understood their destiny.

18   Indeed, you put them in slippery places;
       you make them fall into ruin.

19   How suddenly they become a desolation!
       They come to an end, swept away by terrors.

20   Like one waking from a dream,
       Lord, when arising, you will despise their image.

21   When I became embittered
       and my innermost being was wounded,

22   I was stupid and didn't understand;
       I was an unthinking animal toward you.

23   Yet I am always with you;
       you hold my right hand.

24   You guide me with your counsel,
       and afterward you will take me up in glory.

25   Who do I have in heaven but you?
       And I desire nothing on earth but you.

26   My flesh and my heart may fail,
       but God is the strength of my heart,
       my portion forever.

27   Those far from you will certainly perish;
       you destroy all who are unfaithful to you.

28   But as for me, God's presence is my good.
       I have made the Lord GOD my refuge,
       so I can tell about all you do.

PSALM 74

PRAYER FOR ISRAEL

A Maskil *of Asaph.*

1   Why have you rejected us forever, God?
       Why does your anger burn
       against the sheep of your pasture?

Remember your congregation,
which you purchased long ago
and redeemed as the tribe for
your own possession.

PSALM 74:2

2 Remember your congregation,
which you purchased long ago
and redeemed as the tribe for your own possession.
Remember Mount Zion where you dwell.

3 Make your way to the perpetual ruins,
to all that the enemy has destroyed in the sanctuary.

4 Your adversaries roared in the meeting place
where you met with us.
They set up their emblems as signs.

5 It was like men in a thicket of trees,
wielding axes,

6 then smashing all the carvings
with hatchets and picks.

7 They set your sanctuary on fire;
they utterly desecrated
the dwelling place of your name.

8 They said in their hearts,
"Let's oppress them relentlessly."
They burned every place throughout the land
where God met with us.

9 There are no signs for us to see.
There is no longer a prophet.
And none of us knows how long this will last.

10 God, how long will the enemy mock?
Will the foe insult your name forever?

11 Why do you hold back your hand?
Stretch out your right hand and destroy them!

12 God my King is from ancient times,
performing saving acts on the earth.

13 You divided the sea with your strength;
you smashed the heads of the sea monsters in
the water;

14 you crushed the heads of Leviathan;
you fed him to the creatures of the desert.

15 You opened up springs and streams;
you dried up ever-flowing rivers.

16 The day is yours, also the night;
you established the moon and the sun.

17 You set all the boundaries of the earth;
you made summer and winter.

18 Remember this: the enemy has mocked the LORD,
and a foolish people has insulted your name.

19 Do not give to beasts the life of your dove;
do not forget the lives of your poor people forever.

20 Consider the covenant,
for the dark places of the land are full of violence.

21 Do not let the oppressed turn away in shame;
let the poor and needy praise your name.

22 Rise up, God, champion your cause!
Remember the insults
that fools bring against you all day long.

23 Do not forget the clamor of your adversaries,
the tumult of your opponents that goes up constantly.

DAILY REFLECTION QUESTIONS

III

1 WHAT THEMES DID YOU NOTICE IN TODAY'S PSALMS?

2 WHAT METAPHORS, IMAGERY, OR POETIC DEVICES WERE
USED IN TODAY'S PSALMS TO HIGHLIGHT THESE THEMES?

Emotion
in Psalms

The psalms chosen for this reading plan represent the broader themes and patterns of the book as a whole. The book of Psalms is filled with many expressions of human emotion, and it teaches us how to express our emotions in godly ways through worship. Arranged by category, this list includes some of the many emotions found in the psalms from this Study Book.

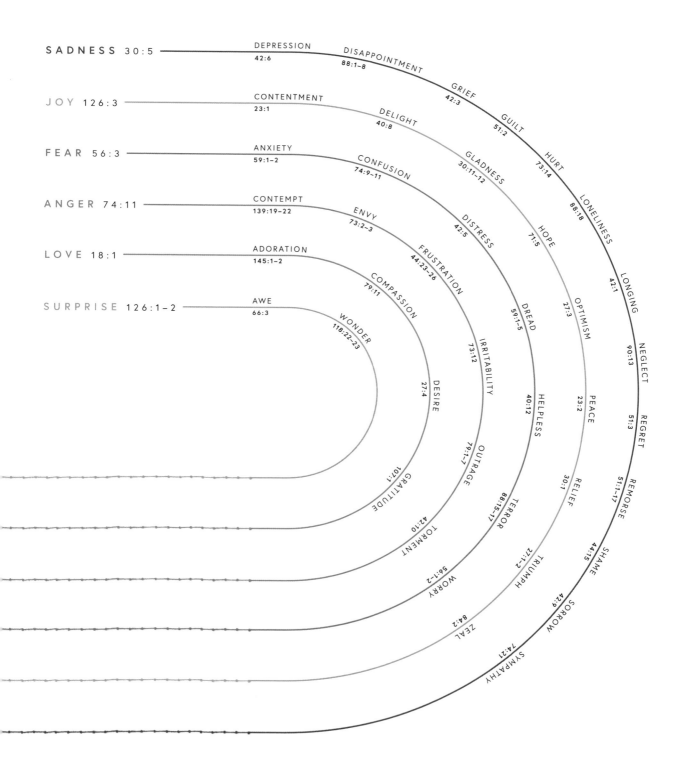

SADNESS 30:5
JOY 126:3
FEAR 56:3
ANGER 74:11
LOVE 18:1
SURPRISE 126:1–2

DEPRESSION 42:6
CONTENTMENT 23:1
ANXIETY 59:1–2
CONTEMPT 139:19–22
ADORATION 145:1–2
AWE 66:3

DISAPPOINTMENT 88:1–8
DELIGHT 40:8
CONFUSION 74:9–11
ENVY 73:2–3
COMPASSION 79:11
WONDER 118:22–23

GRIEF 42:3
GLADNESS 30:11–12
DISTRESS 42:5
FRUSTRATION 44:23–26
DESIRE 27:4
GRATITUDE 107:1

GUILT 51:2
HOPE 71:5
DREAD 59:1–5
IRRITABILITY 73:12
TORMENT 42:10

HURT 73:14
OPTIMISM 27:3
HELPLESS 40:12
OUTRAGE 79:1–7
WORRY 56:1–2

LONELINESS 88:18
PEACE 23:2
TERROR 88:15–17
ZEAL 84:2

LONGING 42:1
RELIEF 30:1
TRIUMPH 27:1–2
SORROW 74:21

NEGLECT 90:13
REGRET 51:3
SHAME 44:15
SYMPATHY

REMORSE 51:11–17

III

Asking God for Restoration

PSALM 79

FAITH AMID CONFUSION

A psalm of Asaph.

¹ God, the nations have invaded your inheritance,
desecrated your holy temple,
and turned Jerusalem into ruins.
² They gave the corpses of your servants
to the birds of the sky for food,
the flesh of your faithful ones
to the beasts of the earth.
³ They poured out their blood
like water all around Jerusalem,
and there was no one to bury them.
⁴ We have become an object of reproach
to our neighbors,
a source of mockery and ridicule
to those around us.

⁵ How long, Lᴏʀᴅ? Will you be angry forever?
Will your jealousy keep burning like fire?
⁶ Pour out your wrath on the nations
that don't acknowledge you,
on the kingdoms that don't call on your name,

7   for they have devoured Jacob
    and devastated his homeland.
8   Do not hold past iniquities against us;
    let your compassion come to us quickly,
    for we have become very weak.

9   God of our salvation, help us,
    for the glory of your name.
    Rescue us and atone for our sins,
    for your name's sake.
10 Why should the nations ask,
    "Where is their God?"
    Before our eyes,
    let vengeance for the shed blood of your servants
    be known among the nations.
11 Let the groans of the prisoners reach you;
    according to your great power,
    preserve those condemned to die.

12 Pay back sevenfold to our neighbors
    the reproach they have hurled at you, Lord.
13 Then we, your people, the sheep of your pasture,
    will thank you forever;
    we will declare your praise
    to generation after generation.

PSALM 80

A PRAYER FOR RESTORATION

*For the choir director: according to "The Lilies." A testimony of
Asaph. A psalm.*

1   Listen, Shepherd of Israel,
    who leads Joseph like a flock;
    you who sit enthroned between the cherubim,
    shine ² on Ephraim,
    Benjamin, and Manasseh.
    Rally your power and come to save us.
3   Restore us, God;
    make your face shine on us,
    so that we may be saved.

4   Lord God of Armies,
    how long will you be angry
    with your people's prayers?

5   You fed them the bread of tears
    and gave them a full measure
    of tears to drink.
6   You put us at odds with our neighbors;
    our enemies mock us.
7   Restore us, God of Armies;
    make your face shine on us, so that we may be saved.

8   You dug up a vine from Egypt;
    you drove out the nations and planted it.
9   You cleared a place for it;
    it took root and filled the land.
10 The mountains were covered by its shade,
    and the mighty cedars with its branches.
11 It sent out sprouts toward the Sea
    and shoots toward the River.

12 Why have you broken down its walls
    so that all who pass by pick its fruit?
13 Boars from the forest tear at it
    and creatures of the field feed on it.
14 Return, God of Armies.
    Look down from heaven and see;
    take care of this vine,
15 the root your right hand planted,
    the son that you made strong for yourself.
16 It was cut down and burned;
    they perish at the rebuke of your countenance.
17 Let your hand be with the man at your right hand,
    with the son of man
    you have made strong for yourself.
18 Then we will not turn away from you;
    revive us, and we will call on your name.
19 Restore us, Lord, God of Armies;
    make your face shine on us, so that we may be saved.

PSALM 81

A CALL TO OBEDIENCE

For the choir director: on the Gittith. *Of Asaph.*

1   Sing for joy to God our strength;
    shout in triumph to the God of Jacob.
2   Lift up a song—play the tambourine,
    the melodious lyre, and the harp.

3   Blow the ram's horn on the day of our feasts
    during the new moon
    and during the full moon.
4   For this is a statute for Israel,
    an ordinance of the God of Jacob.
5   He set it up as a decree for Joseph
    when he went throughout the land of Egypt.
    I heard an unfamiliar language:
6   "I relieved his shoulder from the burden;
    his hands were freed from carrying the basket.
7   You called out in distress, and I rescued you;
    I answered you from the thundercloud.
    I tested you at the Waters of Meribah.   *Selah*
8   Listen, my people, and I will admonish you.
    Israel, if you would only listen to me!
9   There must not be a strange god among you;
    you must not bow down to a foreign god.
10 I am the LORD your God,
    who brought you up from the land of Egypt.
    Open your mouth wide, and I will fill it.

11 "But my people did not listen to my voice;
    Israel did not obey me.
12 So I gave them over to their stubborn hearts
    to follow their own plans.
13 If only my people would listen to me
    and Israel would follow my ways,
14 I would quickly subdue their enemies
    and turn my hand against their foes."
15 Those who hate the LORD

would cower to him;
    their doom would last forever.
16 But he would feed Israel with the best wheat.
    "I would satisfy you with honey from the rock."

PSALM 82

A PLEA FOR RIGHTEOUS JUDGMENT

A psalm of Asaph.

1   God stands in the divine assembly;
    he pronounces judgment among the gods:
2   "How long will you judge unjustly
    and show partiality to the wicked?   *Selah*
3   Provide justice for the needy and the fatherless;
    uphold the rights of the oppressed and the destitute.
4   Rescue the poor and needy;
    save them from the power of the wicked."

5   They do not know or understand;
    they wander in darkness.
    All the foundations of the earth are shaken.

6   I said, "You are gods;
    you are all sons of the Most High.
7   However, you will die like humans
    and fall like any other ruler."

8   Rise up, God, judge the earth,
    for all the nations belong to you.

DAILY REFLECTION QUESTIONS

III

1

WHAT THEMES DID YOU NOTICE IN TODAY'S PSALMS?

2

WHAT METAPHORS, IMAGERY, OR POETIC DEVICES WERE
USED IN TODAY'S PSALMS TO HIGHLIGHT THESE THEMES?

May my prayer reach your presence;
listen to my cry.

PSALM 88:2

Longing for God's Presence

PSALM 84

LONGING FOR GOD'S HOUSE

For the choir director: on the Gittith. *A psalm of the sons of Korah.*

1   How lovely is your dwelling place,
     Lord of Armies.
2   I long and yearn
     for the courts of the Lord;
     my heart and flesh cry out for the living God.

3   Even a sparrow finds a home,
     and a swallow, a nest for herself
     where she places her young—
     near your altars, Lord of Armies,
     my King and my God.
4   How happy are those who reside in your house,
     who praise you continually.   *Selah*

5   Happy are the people whose strength is in you,
     whose hearts are set on pilgrimage.
6   As they pass through the Valley of Baca,
     they make it a source of spring water;
     even the autumn rain will cover it with blessings.

7   They go from strength to strength;
    each appears before God in Zion.

8   LORD God of Armies, hear my prayer;
    listen, God of Jacob.   *Selah*

9   Consider our shield, God;
    look on the face of your anointed one.

10 Better a day in your courts
    than a thousand anywhere else.
    I would rather stand at the threshold of the house
      of my God
    than live in the tents of wicked people.

11 For the LORD God is a sun and shield.
    The LORD grants favor and honor;
    he does not withhold the good
    from those who live with integrity.

12 Happy is the person who trusts in you,
    LORD of Armies!

PSALMS 88–89

Book III ends with
Psalm 88, which
many consider
the saddest and
grimmest psalm, and
Psalm 89, a lament.

PSALM 88

A CRY OF DESPERATION

A song. A psalm of the sons of Korah. For the choir director: according to Mahalath Leannoth. *A Maskil of Heman the Ezrahite.*

1   LORD, God of my salvation,
    I cry out before you day and night.

2   May my prayer reach your presence;
    listen to my cry.

3   For I have had enough troubles,
    and my life is near Sheol.

4   I am counted among those going down to the Pit.
    I am like a man without strength,

5   abandoned among the dead.
    I am like the slain lying in the grave,
    whom you no longer remember,
    and who are cut off from your care.

6   You have put me in the lowest part of the Pit,
    in the darkest places, in the depths.

7   Your wrath weighs heavily on me;
    you have overwhelmed me with all your waves.   *Selah*

8 You have distanced my friends from me;
 you have made me repulsive to them.
 I am shut in and cannot go out.
9 My eyes are worn out from crying.
 Lord, I cry out to you all day long;
 I spread out my hands to you.

10 Do you work wonders for the dead?
 Do departed spirits rise up to praise you?   *Selah*
11 Will your faithful love be declared in the grave,
 your faithfulness in Abaddon?
12 Will your wonders be known in the darkness
 or your righteousness in the land of oblivion?

13 But I call to you for help, Lord;
 in the morning my prayer meets you.
14 Lord, why do you reject me?
 Why do you hide your face from me?
15 From my youth,
 I have been suffering and near death.
 I suffer your horrors; I am desperate.
16 Your wrath sweeps over me;
 your terrors destroy me.
17 They surround me like water all day long;
 they close in on me from every side.
18 You have distanced loved one and neighbor from me;
 darkness is my only friend.

PSALM 89

PERPLEXITY ABOUT GOD'S PROMISES

A Maskil of Ethan the Ezrahite.

1 I will sing about the Lord's faithful love forever;
 I will proclaim your faithfulness to all generations
 with my mouth.
2 For I will declare,
 "Faithful love is built up forever;
 you establish your faithfulness in the heavens."

3 The Lord said,
 "I have made a covenant with my chosen one;
 I have sworn an oath to David my servant:
4 'I will establish your offspring forever
 and build up your throne for all generations.'"   *Selah*

5 Lord, the heavens praise your wonders—
 your faithfulness also—
 in the assembly of the holy ones.
6 For who in the skies can compare with the Lord?
 Who among the heavenly beings is like the Lord?
7 God is greatly feared in the council of the holy ones,
 more awe-inspiring than all who surround him.
8 Lord God of Armies,
 who is strong like you, Lord?
 Your faithfulness surrounds you.
9 You rule the raging sea;
 when its waves surge, you still them.
10 You crushed Rahab like one who is slain;
 you scattered your enemies with your powerful arm.
11 The heavens are yours; the earth also is yours.
 The world and everything in it—you founded them.
12 North and south—you created them.
 Tabor and Hermon shout for joy at your name.
13 You have a mighty arm;
 your hand is powerful;
 your right hand is lifted high.
14 Righteousness and justice are the foundation
 of your throne;
 faithful love and truth go before you.
15 Happy are the people who know the joyful shout;
 Lord, they walk in the light from your face.
16 They rejoice in your name all day long,
 and they are exalted by your righteousness.
17 For you are their magnificent strength;
 by your favor our horn is exalted.
18 Surely our shield belongs to the Lord,
 our king to the Holy One of Israel.

19 You once spoke in a vision to your faithful ones
 and said, "I have granted help to a warrior;
 I have exalted one chosen from the people.
20 I have found David my servant;
 I have anointed him with my sacred oil.
21 My hand will always be with him,
 and my arm will strengthen him.
22 The enemy will not oppress him;
 the wicked will not afflict him.
23 I will crush his foes before him
 and strike those who hate him.

24 My faithfulness and love will be with him,
    and through my name
    his horn will be exalted.
25 I will extend his power to the sea
    and his right hand to the rivers.
26 He will call to me, 'You are my Father,
    my God, the rock of my salvation.'
27 I will also make him my firstborn,
    greatest of the kings of the earth.
28 I will always preserve my faithful love for him,
    and my covenant with him will endure.
29 I will establish his line forever,
    his throne as long as heaven lasts.
30 If his sons abandon my instruction
    and do not live by my ordinances,
31 if they dishonor my statutes
    and do not keep my commands,
32 then I will call their rebellion
    to account with the rod,
    their iniquity with blows.
33 But I will not withdraw
    my faithful love from him
    or betray my faithfulness.
34 I will not violate my covenant
    or change what my lips have said.
35 Once and for all
    I have sworn an oath by my holiness;
    I will not lie to David.
36 His offspring will continue forever,
    his throne like the sun before me,
37 like the moon, established forever,
    a faithful witness in the sky." *Selah*

38 But you have spurned and rejected him;
    you have become enraged with your anointed.
39 You have repudiated the covenant with your servant;
    you have completely dishonored his crown.
40 You have broken down all his walls;
    you have reduced his fortified cities to ruins.
41 All who pass by plunder him;
    he has become an object of ridicule
    to his neighbors.
42 You have lifted high the right hand of his foes;
    you have made all his enemies rejoice.

43 You have also turned back his sharp sword
    and have not let him stand in battle.
44 You have made his splendor cease
    and have overturned his throne.
45 You have shortened the days of his youth;
    you have covered him with shame. *Selah*

46 How long, LORD? Will you hide forever?
    Will your anger keep burning like fire?
47 Remember how short my life is.
    Have you created everyone for nothing?
48 What courageous person can live and never see death?
    Who can save himself from the power of
        Sheol? *Selah*
49 Lord, where are the former acts of your faithful love
    that you swore to David in your faithfulness?
50 Remember, Lord, the ridicule against your servants—
    in my heart I carry abuse from all the peoples—
51 how your enemies have ridiculed, LORD,
    how they have ridiculed every step of your anointed.

52 Blessed be the LORD forever.
    Amen and amen.

DAILY REFLECTION QUESTIONS

1

WHAT THEMES DID YOU NOTICE IN TODAY'S PSALMS?

2

WHAT METAPHORS, IMAGERY, OR POETIC DEVICES WERE
USED IN TODAY'S PSALMS TO HIGHLIGHT THESE THEMES?

BOOK

III

Response

1

LOOK BACK AT YOUR DAILY REFLECTIONS. HOW DO EACH OF THE THEMES YOU NOTED CONTRIBUTE TO THE OVERALL MESSAGE OF BOOK III?

LOOK BACK AT PAGE 72 IF YOU NEED A REMINDER.

2

HOW DO THESE THEMES ANTICIPATE JESUS, THE ETERNAL KING?

3

HOW IS GOD DESCRIBED IN BOOK III?

4

WHAT DO THE PSALMS IN BOOK III MODEL FOR YOU AS A WORSHIPER?

Grace Day

• •

Take this day to catch up on your reading, pray,
and rest in the presence of the Lord.

Therefore, through him let us continually offer up to God a sacrifice of praise, that is, the fruit of lips that confess his name.

HEBREWS 13:15

Weekly
Truth

〰〰〰〰〰〰〰〰〰〰〰〰〰〰〰〰〰〰〰〰〰〰〰〰〰

Scripture is God-breathed and true. When we memorize it, we carry His Word with us wherever we go.

This week, we will memorize the last two lines from Psalm 40:3, where David praises God for His deliverance.

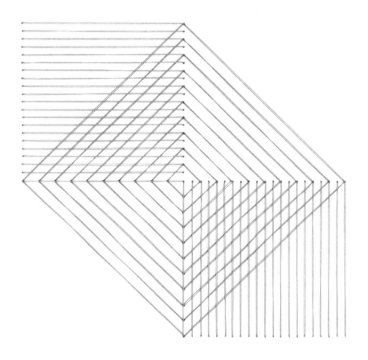

HE PUT A NEW SONG IN MY MOUTH,
A HYMN OF PRAISE TO OUR GOD.
**MANY WILL SEE AND FEAR,
AND THEY WILL TRUST IN THE LORD.**

PSALM 40:3

See tips for memorizing Scripture on page 144.

BOOK

IV

Psalms 90–106

INTRODUCTION

Book IV is a response to the despair of Book III. With only two psalms attributed to David, this section anchors the worshiper outside the reign of David, all the way back to creation, the exodus, and the early history of the nation of Israel. These psalms remind the worshiper that the Lord reigns, has always reigned, and will continue to reign, even when an unrighteous king has been on the throne. The Lord is the true King who will establish His throne on earth and deliver His people. This collection concludes with a call to gather God's people from among the nations so they too can praise Him.

/\

KEY FACTS

1 This book begins with a psalm attributed to Moses, which is thought to be the oldest psalm in the Psalter.

2 The psalms in Book IV have a corporate or liturgical emphasis.

3 This book contains many psalms called enthronement psalms that declare "The Lord reigns."

God Reigns

DAY 15

Forever

Book IV responds to
the despair of Book III
by pointing to God's
eternal reign.

PSALM 90

ETERNAL GOD AND MORTAL MAN

A prayer of Moses, the man of God.

1   Lord, you have been our refuge
    in every generation.
2   Before the mountains were born,
    before you gave birth to the earth and the world,
    from eternity to eternity, you are God.

3   You return mankind to the dust,
    saying, "Return, descendants of Adam."
4   For in your sight a thousand years
    are like yesterday that passes by,
    like a few hours of the night.
5   You end their lives; they sleep.
    They are like grass that grows in the morning—
6   in the morning it sprouts and grows;
    by evening it withers and dries up.

7   For we are consumed by your anger;
    we are terrified by your wrath.
8   You have set our iniquities before you,
    our secret sins in the light of your presence.
9   For all our days ebb away under your wrath;
    we end our years like a sigh.
10 Our lives last seventy years
    or, if we are strong, eighty years.
    Even the best of them are struggle and sorrow;
    indeed, they pass quickly and we fly away.
11 Who understands the power of your anger?
    Your wrath matches the fear that is due you.
12 Teach us to number our days carefully
    so that we may develop wisdom in our hearts.

13 Lord—how long?
    Turn and have compassion on your servants.
14 Satisfy us in the morning with your faithful love
    so that we may shout with joy and be glad all our days.
15 Make us rejoice for as many days as you have humbled us,
    for as many years as we have seen adversity.
16 Let your work be seen by your servants,
    and your splendor by their children.
17 Let the favor of the Lord our God be on us;
    establish for us the work of our hands—
    establish the work of our hands!

Your throne has been established
from the beginning;
you are from eternity.

PSALM 93:2

PSALM 91

THE PROTECTION OF THE MOST HIGH

1 The one who lives under the protection of the
   Most High
   dwells in the shadow of the Almighty.

2 I will say concerning the LORD, who is my refuge
   and my fortress,
   my God in whom I trust:

3 He himself will rescue you from the bird trap,
   from the destructive plague.

4 He will cover you with his feathers;
   you will take refuge under his wings.
   His faithfulness will be a protective shield.

5 You will not fear the terror of the night,
   the arrow that flies by day,

6 the plague that stalks in darkness,
   or the pestilence that ravages at noon.

7 Though a thousand fall at your side
   and ten thousand at your right hand,
   the pestilence will not reach you.

8 You will only see it with your eyes
   and witness the punishment of the wicked.

9 Because you have made the LORD—my refuge,
   the Most High—your dwelling place,

10 no harm will come to you;
    no plague will come near your tent.

11 For he will give his angels orders concerning you,
    to protect you in all your ways.

12 They will support you with their hands
    so that you will not strike your foot against a stone.

13 You will tread on the lion and the cobra;
    you will trample the young lion and the serpent.

14 Because he has his heart set on me,
    I will deliver him;
    I will protect him because he knows my name.

15 When he calls out to me, I will answer him;
    I will be with him in trouble.
    I will rescue him and give him honor.

16 I will satisfy him with a long life
    and show him my salvation.

PSALM 92

GOD'S LOVE AND FAITHFULNESS

A psalm. A song for the Sabbath day.

1 It is good to give thanks to the LORD,
   to sing praise to your name, Most High,

2 to declare your faithful love in the morning
   and your faithfulness at night,

3 with a ten-stringed harp
   and the music of a lyre.

4 For you have made me rejoice, LORD,
   by what you have done;

I will shout for joy
because of the works of your hands.
5   How magnificent are your works, LORD,
how profound your thoughts!
6   A stupid person does not know,
a fool does not understand this:
7   though the wicked sprout like grass
and all evildoers flourish,
they will be eternally destroyed.
8   But you, LORD, are exalted forever.
9   For indeed, LORD, your enemies—
indeed, your enemies will perish;
all evildoers will be scattered.
10 You have lifted up my horn
like that of a wild ox;
I have been anointed with the finest oil.
11 My eyes look at my enemies;
when evildoers rise against me,
my ears hear them.

12 The righteous thrive like a palm tree
and grow like a cedar tree in Lebanon.
13 Planted in the house of the LORD,
they thrive in the courts of our God.
14 They will still bear fruit in old age,
healthy and green,
15 to declare, "The LORD is just;
he is my rock,
and there is no unrighteousness in him."

PSALM 93

GOD'S ETERNAL REIGN

1   The LORD reigns! He is robed in majesty;
the LORD is robed, enveloped in strength.
The world is firmly established;
it cannot be shaken.
2   Your throne has been established
from the beginning;
you are from eternity.
3   The floods have lifted up, LORD,
the floods have lifted up their voice;
the floods lift up their pounding waves.

⁴   Greater than the roar of a huge torrent—
     the mighty breakers of the sea—
     the LORD on high is majestic.

⁵   LORD, your testimonies are completely reliable;
     holiness adorns your house
     for all the days to come.

PSALM 95
WORSHIP AND WARNING

¹   Come, let's shout joyfully to the LORD,
     shout triumphantly to the rock of our salvation!
²   Let's enter his presence with thanksgiving;
     let's shout triumphantly to him in song.

³   For the LORD is a great God,
     a great King above all gods.
⁴   The depths of the earth are in his hand,
     and the mountain peaks are his.
⁵   The sea is his; he made it.
     His hands formed the dry land.

⁶   Come, let's worship and bow down;
     let's kneel before the LORD our Maker.
⁷   For he is our God,
     and we are the people of his pasture,
     the sheep under his care.
     Today, if you hear his voice:
⁸   Do not harden your hearts as at Meribah,
     as on that day at Massah in the wilderness
⁹   where your ancestors tested me;
     they tried me, though they had seen what I did.
¹⁰   For forty years I was disgusted with that generation;
     I said, "They are a people whose hearts go astray;
     they do not know my ways."
¹¹   So I swore in my anger,
     "They will not enter my rest."

PSALM 99
THE KING IS HOLY

¹   The LORD reigns! Let the peoples tremble.
     He is enthroned between the cherubim.
     Let the earth quake.
²   The LORD is great in Zion;
     he is exalted above all the peoples.
³   Let them praise your great
     and awe-inspiring name.
     He is holy.

⁴   The mighty King loves justice.
     You have established fairness;
     you have administered justice
     and righteousness in Jacob.
⁵   Exalt the LORD our God;
     bow in worship at his footstool.
     He is holy.

⁶   Moses and Aaron were among his priests;
     Samuel also was among those calling on his name.
     They called to the LORD and he answered them.
⁷   He spoke to them in a pillar of cloud;
     they kept his decrees and the statutes he gave them.
⁸   LORD our God, you answered them.
     You were a forgiving God to them,
     but an avenger of their sinful actions.

⁹   Exalt the LORD our God;
     bow in worship at his holy mountain,
     for the LORD our God is holy.

DAILY REFLECTION QUESTIONS

1

WHAT THEMES DID YOU NOTICE IN TODAY'S PSALMS?

2

WHAT METAPHORS, IMAGERY, OR POETIC DEVICES WERE
USED IN TODAY'S PSALMS TO HIGHLIGHT THESE THEMES?

God Cares for His People

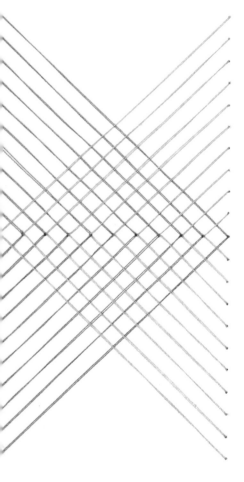

PSALMS 103, 105–106

———

Book IV closes with a call to praise God for His faithful care of His creation.

PSALM 103

THE FORGIVING GOD

Of David.

¹ My soul, bless the LORD,
    and all that is within me, bless his holy name.
² My soul, bless the LORD,
    and do not forget all his benefits.

³ He forgives all your iniquity;
    he heals all your diseases.
⁴ He redeems your life from the Pit;
    he crowns you with faithful love and compassion.
⁵ He satisfies you with good things;
    your youth is renewed like the eagle.

⁶ The LORD executes acts of righteousness
    and justice for all the oppressed.
⁷ He revealed his ways to Moses,
    his deeds to the people of Israel.
⁸ The LORD is compassionate and gracious,
    slow to anger and abounding in faithful love.
⁹ He will not always accuse us
    or be angry forever.
¹⁰ He has not dealt with us as our sins deserve
    or repaid us according to our iniquities.

¹¹ For as high as the heavens are above the earth,
    so great is his faithful love
    toward those who fear him.

¹² As far as the east is from the west,
so far has he removed
our transgressions from us.
¹³ As a father has compassion on his children,
so the LORD has compassion on those who fear him.
¹⁴ For he knows what we are made of,
remembering that we are dust.

¹⁵ As for man, his days are like grass—
he blooms like a flower of the field;
¹⁶ when the wind passes over it, it vanishes,
and its place is no longer known.
¹⁷ But from eternity to eternity
the LORD's faithful love is toward those who fear him,
and his righteousness toward the grandchildren
¹⁸ of those who keep his covenant,
who remember to observe his precepts.
¹⁹ The LORD has established his throne in heaven,
and his kingdom rules over all.

²⁰ Bless the LORD,
all his angels of great strength,
who do his word,
obedient to his command.
²¹ Bless the LORD, all his armies,
his servants who do his will.
²² Bless the LORD, all his works
in all the places where he rules.
My soul, bless the LORD!

PSALM 105

GOD'S FAITHFULNESS TO HIS PEOPLE

¹ Give thanks to the LORD, call on his name;
proclaim his deeds among the peoples.
² Sing to him, sing praise to him;
tell about all his wondrous works!
³ Boast in his holy name;
let the hearts of those who seek the LORD rejoice.
⁴ Seek the LORD and his strength;
seek his face always.
⁵ Remember the wondrous works he has done,
his wonders, and the judgments he has pronounced,
⁶ you offspring of Abraham his servant,
Jacob's descendants—his chosen ones.

⁷ He is the LORD our God;
his judgments govern the whole earth.
⁸ He remembers his covenant forever,
the promise he ordained
for a thousand generations—
⁹ the covenant he made with Abraham,
swore to Isaac,
¹⁰ and confirmed to Jacob as a decree
and to Israel as a permanent covenant:
¹¹ "I will give the land of Canaan to you
as your inherited portion."

¹² When they were few in number,
very few indeed,
and resident aliens in Canaan,
¹³ wandering from nation to nation
and from one kingdom to another,
¹⁴ he allowed no one to oppress them;
he rebuked kings on their behalf:
¹⁵ "Do not touch my anointed ones,
or harm my prophets."

¹⁶ He called down famine against the land
and destroyed the entire food supply.
¹⁷ He had sent a man ahead of them—
Joseph, who was sold as a slave.
¹⁸ They hurt his feet with shackles;
his neck was put in an iron collar.
¹⁹ Until the time his prediction came true,
the word of the LORD tested him.
²⁰ The king sent for him and released him;
the ruler of peoples set him free.
²¹ He made him master of his household,
ruler over all his possessions—
²² binding his officials at will
and instructing his elders.

²³ Then Israel went to Egypt;
Jacob lived as an alien in the land of Ham.
²⁴ The LORD made his people very fruitful;
he made them more numerous than their foes,
²⁵ whose hearts he turned to hate his people
and to deal deceptively with his servants.
²⁶ He sent Moses his servant,
and Aaron, whom he had chosen.

> *But from eternity to eternity*
> *the L*ord*'s faithful love is toward*
> *those who fear him.*

PSALM 103:17

27 They performed his miraculous signs among them
and wonders in the land of Ham.

28 He sent darkness, and it became dark—
for did they not defy his commands?

29 He turned their water into blood
and caused their fish to die.

30 Their land was overrun with frogs,
even in their royal chambers.

31 He spoke, and insects came—
gnats throughout their country.

32 He gave them hail for rain,
and lightning throughout their land.

33 He struck their vines and fig trees
and shattered the trees of their territory.

34 He spoke, and locusts came—
young locusts without number.

35 They devoured all the vegetation in their land
and consumed the produce of their land.

36 He struck all the firstborn in their land,
all their first progeny.

37 Then he brought Israel out with silver and gold,
and no one among his tribes stumbled.

38 Egypt was glad when they left,
for the dread of Israel had fallen on them.

39 He spread a cloud as a covering
and gave a fire to light up the night.

40 They asked, and he brought quail
and satisfied them with bread from heaven.

41 He opened a rock, and water gushed out;
it flowed like a stream in the desert.

42 For he remembered his holy promise
to Abraham his servant.

43 He brought his people out with rejoicing,
his chosen ones with shouts of joy.

44 He gave them the lands of the nations,
and they inherited
what other peoples had worked for.

45 All this happened
so that they might keep his statutes
and obey his instructions.
Hallelujah!

PSALM 106

ISRAEL'S UNFAITHFULNESS TO GOD

1 Hallelujah!
Give thanks to the Lord, for he is good;
his faithful love endures forever.

2 Who can declare the Lord's mighty acts
or proclaim all the praise due him?

3 How happy are those who uphold justice,
who practice righteousness at all times.

106 AMEN AND AMEN: A JOURNEY THROUGH THE PSALMS

4   Remember me, LORD,
        when you show favor to your people.
        Come to me with your salvation
5   so that I may enjoy the prosperity
        of your chosen ones,
        rejoice in the joy of your nation,
        and boast about your heritage.

6   Both we and our ancestors have sinned;
        we have done wrong and have acted wickedly.
7   Our ancestors in Egypt did not grasp
        the significance of your wondrous works
        or remember your many acts of faithful love;
        instead, they rebelled by the sea—the Red Sea.
8   Yet he saved them for his name's sake,
        to make his power known.
9   He rebuked the Red Sea, and it dried up;
        he led them through the depths as through a desert.
10   He saved them from the power of the adversary;
        he redeemed them from the power of the enemy.
11   Water covered their foes;
        not one of them remained.
12   Then they believed his promises
        and sang his praise.

13   They soon forgot his works
        and would not wait for his counsel.
14   They were seized with craving in the wilderness
        and tested God in the desert.
15   He gave them what they asked for,
        but sent a wasting disease among them.

16   In the camp they were envious of Moses
        and of Aaron, the LORD's holy one.
17   The earth opened up and swallowed Dathan;
        it covered the assembly of Abiram.
18   Fire blazed throughout their assembly;
        flames consumed the wicked.

19   At Horeb they made a calf
        and worshiped the cast metal image.
20   They exchanged their glory
        for the image of a grass-eating ox.

21 They forgot God their Savior,
  who did great things in Egypt,
22 wondrous works in the land of Ham,
  awe-inspiring acts at the Red Sea.
23 So he said he would have destroyed them—
  if Moses his chosen one
  had not stood before him in the breach
  to turn his wrath away from destroying them.

24 They despised the pleasant land
  and did not believe his promise.
25 They grumbled in their tents
  and did not listen to the LORD.
26 So he raised his hand against them with an oath
  that he would make them fall in the desert
27 and would disperse their descendants
  among the nations,
  scattering them throughout the lands.

28 They aligned themselves with Baal of Peor
  and ate sacrifices offered to lifeless gods.
29 They angered the LORD with their deeds,
  and a plague broke out against them.
30 But Phinehas stood up and intervened,
  and the plague was stopped.
31 It was credited to him as righteousness
  throughout all generations to come.

32 They angered the LORD at the Waters of Meribah,
  and Moses suffered because of them,
33 for they embittered his spirit,
  and he spoke rashly with his lips.

34 They did not destroy the peoples
  as the LORD had commanded them
35 but mingled with the nations
  and adopted their ways.
36 They served their idols,
  which became a snare to them.

37 They sacrificed their sons and daughters to demons.
38 They shed innocent blood—
  the blood of their sons and daughters
  whom they sacrificed to the idols of Canaan;
  so the land became polluted with blood.
39 They defiled themselves by their actions
  and prostituted themselves by their deeds.

40 Therefore the LORD's anger burned against his people,
  and he abhorred his own inheritance.
41 He handed them over to the nations;
  those who hated them ruled over them.
42 Their enemies oppressed them,
  and they were subdued under their power.
43 He rescued them many times,
  but they continued to rebel deliberately
  and were beaten down by their iniquity.

44 When he heard their cry,
  he took note of their distress,
45 remembered his covenant with them,
  and relented according to the abundance
  of his faithful love.
46 He caused them to be pitied
  before all their captors.

47 Save us, LORD our God,
  and gather us from the nations,
  so that we may give thanks to your holy name
  and rejoice in your praise.

48 Blessed be the LORD God of Israel,
  from everlasting to everlasting.
  Let all the people say, "Amen!"
  Hallelujah!

DAILY REFLECTION QUESTIONS

IV

1

WHAT THEMES DID YOU NOTICE IN TODAY'S PSALMS?

2

WHAT METAPHORS, IMAGERY, OR POETIC DEVICES WERE
USED IN TODAY'S PSALMS TO HIGHLIGHT THESE THEMES?

BOOK

IV

Response

1

LOOK BACK AT YOUR DAILY REFLECTIONS. HOW DO EACH OF THE THEMES YOU NOTED CONTRIBUTE TO THE OVERALL MESSAGE OF BOOK IV?

LOOK BACK AT PAGE 97 IF YOU NEED A REMINDER.

2

HOW DO THESE THEMES ANTICIPATE JESUS, THE ETERNAL KING?

3

HOW IS GOD DESCRIBED IN BOOK IV?

4

WHAT DO THE PSALMS IN BOOK IV MODEL FOR YOU AS A WORSHIPER?

BOOK

V

Psalms 107–150

INTRODUCTION

The plea in Psalm 106:47 that ends Book IV is answered in the first psalm of Book V. The rest of this section is an invitation to exuberant praise and worship in light of God's covenant love, His Word, and the reminder that His promise of David's neverending throne would be fulfilled in the Messiah. It includes several psalms testifying to God's rule and reign. The entire Psalter concludes here in Book V with five psalms of climactic, resounding praise.

KEY FACTS

1 Like Book IV, this section carries a corporate or liturgical tone.

2 Psalm 119, the longest psalm in the Psalter, is an extended reflection on the importance of God's Word.

3 Psalms 113–118, known as the Egyptian Hallel, were traditionally sung during Passover. It is likely that Jesus would have sung these songs during the Last Supper.

4 Psalms 120–134 are known as the Psalms of Ascent. These prayers were sung on the way to festivals in Jerusalem.

The Faithful Love of God

PSALM 107

THANKSGIVING FOR GOD'S DELIVERANCE

1   Give thanks to the Lord, for he is good;
    his faithful love endures forever.
2   Let the redeemed of the Lord proclaim
    that he has redeemed them from the power of the foe
3   and has gathered them from the lands—
    from the east and the west,
    from the north and the south.

4   Some wandered in the desolate wilderness,
    finding no way to a city where they could live.
5   They were hungry and thirsty;
    their spirits failed within them.
6   Then they cried out to the Lord in their trouble;
    he rescued them from their distress.
7   He led them by the right path
    to go to a city where they could live.
8   Let them give thanks to the Lord
    for his faithful love
    and his wondrous works for all humanity.
9   For he has satisfied the thirsty
    and filled the hungry with good things.

Give thanks to the Lord, for he is good;
his faithful love endures forever.

PSALM 118:1

¹⁰ Others sat in darkness and gloom—
prisoners in cruel chains—

¹¹ because they rebelled against God's commands
and despised the counsel of the Most High.

¹² He broke their spirits with hard labor;
they stumbled, and there was no one to help.

¹³ Then they cried out to the Lord in their trouble;
he saved them from their distress.

¹⁴ He brought them out of darkness and gloom
and broke their chains apart.

¹⁵ Let them give thanks to the Lord
for his faithful love
and his wondrous works for all humanity.

¹⁶ For he has broken down the bronze gates
and cut through the iron bars.

¹⁷ Fools suffered affliction
because of their rebellious ways and their iniquities.

¹⁸ They loathed all food
and came near the gates of death.

¹⁹ Then they cried out to the Lord in their trouble;
he saved them from their distress.

²⁰ He sent his word and healed them;
he rescued them from their traps.

²¹ Let them give thanks to the Lord
for his faithful love
and his wondrous works for all humanity.

²² Let them offer thanksgiving sacrifices
and announce his works with shouts of joy.

²³ Others went to sea in ships,
conducting trade on the vast water.

²⁴ They saw the Lord's works,
his wondrous works in the deep.

²⁵ He spoke and raised a stormy wind
that stirred up the waves of the sea.

²⁶ Rising up to the sky, sinking down to the depths,
their courage melting away in anguish,

²⁷ they reeled and staggered like a drunkard,
and all their skill was useless.

²⁸ Then they cried out to the Lord in their trouble,
and he brought them out of their distress.

²⁹ He stilled the storm to a whisper,
and the waves of the sea were hushed.

³⁰ They rejoiced when the waves grew quiet.
Then he guided them to the harbor they longed for.

³¹ Let them give thanks to the Lord
for his faithful love
and his wondrous works for all humanity.

³² Let them exalt him in the assembly of the people
and praise him in the council of the elders.

³³ He turns rivers into desert,
springs into thirsty ground,

³⁴ and fruitful land into salty wasteland,
because of the wickedness of its inhabitants.

³⁵ He turns a desert into a pool,
dry land into springs.

³⁶ He causes the hungry to settle there,
and they establish a city where they can live.

37   They sow fields and plant vineyards
        that yield a fruitful harvest.
38   He blesses them, and they multiply greatly;
        he does not let their livestock decrease.

39   When they are diminished and are humbled
        by cruel oppression and sorrow,
40   he pours contempt on nobles
        and makes them wander in a trackless wasteland.
41   But he lifts the needy out of their suffering
        and makes their families multiply like flocks.
42   The upright see it and rejoice,
        and all injustice shuts its mouth.

43   Let whoever is wise pay attention to these things
        and consider the LORD's acts of faithful love.

PSALM 110

———

This royal psalm
looks beyond
David's reign to the
promised Messiah.

PSALM 110

THE PRIESTLY KING

A psalm of David.

1   This is the declaration of the LORD
        to my Lord:
        "Sit at my right hand
        until I make your enemies your footstool."
2   The LORD will extend your mighty scepter from Zion.
        Rule over your surrounding enemies.
3   Your people will volunteer
        on your day of battle.
        In holy splendor, from the womb of the dawn,
        the dew of your youth belongs to you.
4   The LORD has sworn an oath and will not take it back:
        "You are a priest forever
        according to the pattern of Melchizedek."

5   The Lord is at your right hand;
        he will crush kings on the day of his anger.
6   He will judge the nations, heaping up corpses;
        he will crush leaders over the entire world.
7   He will drink from the brook by the road;
        therefore, he will lift up his head.

PSALM 118

1 Give thanks to the LORD, for he is good;
his faithful love endures forever.

2 Let Israel say,
"His faithful love endures forever."

3 Let the house of Aaron say,
"His faithful love endures forever."

4 Let those who fear the LORD say,
"His faithful love endures forever."

5 I called to the LORD in distress;
the LORD answered me
and put me in a spacious place.

6 The LORD is for me; I will not be afraid.
What can a mere mortal do to me?

7 The LORD is my helper;
therefore, I will look in triumph on those who
hate me.

8 It is better to take refuge in the LORD
than to trust in humanity.

9 It is better to take refuge in the LORD
than to trust in nobles.

10 All the nations surrounded me;
in the name of the LORD I destroyed them.

11 They surrounded me, yes, they surrounded me;
in the name of the LORD I destroyed them.

12 They surrounded me like bees;
they were extinguished like a fire among thorns;
in the name of the LORD I destroyed them.

13 They pushed me hard to make me fall,
but the LORD helped me.

14 The LORD is my strength and my song;
he has become my salvation.

15 There are shouts of joy and victory
in the tents of the righteous:
"The LORD's right hand performs valiantly!

16 The LORD's right hand is raised.
The LORD's right hand performs valiantly!"

17 I will not die, but I will live
and proclaim what the LORD has done.

18 The LORD disciplined me severely
but did not give me over to death.

19 Open the gates of righteousness for me;
I will enter through them
and give thanks to the LORD.

20 This is the LORD's gate;
the righteous will enter through it.

21 I will give thanks to you
because you have answered me
and have become my salvation.

22 The stone that the builders rejected
has become the cornerstone.

23 This came from the LORD;
it is wondrous in our sight.

24 This is the day the LORD has made;
let's rejoice and be glad in it.

25 LORD, save us!
LORD, please grant us success!

26 He who comes in the name
of the LORD is blessed.
From the house of the LORD we bless you.

27 The LORD is God and has given us light.
Bind the festival sacrifice with cords
to the horns of the altar.

28 You are my God, and I will give you thanks.
You are my God; I will exalt you.

29 Give thanks to the LORD, for he is good;
his faithful love endures forever.

DAILY REFLECTION QUESTIONS

1

WHAT THEMES DID YOU NOTICE IN TODAY'S PSALMS?

2

WHAT METAPHORS, IMAGERY, OR POETIC DEVICES WERE
USED IN TODAY'S PSALMS TO HIGHLIGHT THESE THEMES?

Major Categories
Within Psalms

Because the book of Psalms is made up of 150 individual psalms, many categories, genres, and forms, ranging in size and scope, have been identified over time to help us better understand the context and intent of the original writers. While some psalms belong to one category alone, many psalms contain overlapping genres. Here you will find an overview of a few of the broad, commonly agreed upon categories of psalms, along with an example of each.

Enthronement Psalms

These psalms focus on and celebrate the kingship and rule of God over not only Israel, but all of creation. They often use phrases such as "Yahweh reigns" and rely heavily on royal imagery and metaphorical language to describe the Lord's position of power. Other categories that fall under enthronement psalms include royal and messianic psalms.

See Psalm 99 on page 102 as an example.

Historical Psalms

The historical psalms appear in two unique forms. First, they include psalms that reflect God's ongoing work throughout history, especially in the life of Israel and Judah. Second, they demonstrate the psalmist's response to specific circumstances in their life, often noted in the superscription before the psalm begins. Many of these psalms correspond to events in David's life.

See Psalm 105 on page 105 as an example.

Imprecatory Psalms

Many of the prayers found within the book of Psalms present requests to God to defeat, and sometimes curse, enemies. These prayers of lament focus on enemies who have committed unspeakable acts of violence against God's people and desecrated sacred places. They give voice to the desire to see evil defeated, justice prevail, and suffering cease.

See Psalm 59 on page 53 as an example.

Lament Psalms

Individual and communal cries to God appear in Scripture in the form of lament psalms. These psalms not only express grief or despair, but also declare faith in God's ability to save and deliver. Other categories that can fall under lament psalms include ascent, messianic, trust, penitential, and Zion psalms.

See Psalm 42 on page 46 as an example.

Praise
Psalms

While the entirety of the Psalter demonstrates praise, specific psalms praise God for His character and actions, or praise Him in light of the individual circumstances the psalmists have experienced Him in. More specifically, some praise psalms are distinguished by opening with the Hebrew word *halal* (meaning "hallelujah"). Other categories that can fall under praise psalms include ascent, confidence, temple entry, thanksgiving, Torah, and Zion psalms.

See Psalm 146 on page 132 as an example.

Wisdom
Psalms

Similar to Job, Proverbs, and Ecclesiastes, the wisdom psalms encourage personal contemplation on life and faith. These psalms encourage the reader to meditate on and respond to God's Word. They are reflections more than prayers, guiding us to consider our lives and struggles. Torah psalms can also fall under this category.

See Psalm 1 on page 25 as an example.

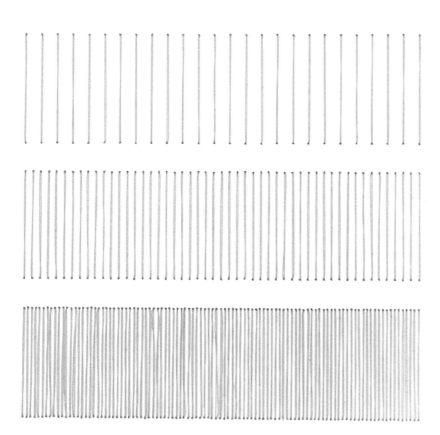

*The LORD will protect your coming and going
both now and forever.*

PSALM 121:8

The Presence of God

PSALM 121

THE LORD OUR PROTECTOR

A song of ascents.

¹ I lift my eyes toward the mountains.
  Where will my help come from?
² My help comes from the LORD,
  the Maker of heaven and earth.

³ He will not allow your foot to slip;
  your Protector will not slumber.
⁴ Indeed, the Protector of Israel
  does not slumber or sleep.

⁵ The LORD protects you;
  the LORD is a shelter right by your side.
⁶ The sun will not strike you by day
  or the moon by night.

⁷ The LORD will protect you from all harm;
  he will protect your life.
⁸ The LORD will protect your coming and going
  both now and forever.

> *For there is faithful love with the LORD,*
> *and with him is redemption in abundance.*
>
> PSALM 130:7

PSALM 123

LOOKING FOR GOD'S FAVOR

A song of ascents.

1 I lift my eyes to you,
the one enthroned in heaven.
2 Like a servant's eyes on his master's hand,
like a servant girl's eyes on her mistress's hand,
so our eyes are on the LORD our God
until he shows us favor.

3 Show us favor, LORD, show us favor,
for we've had more than enough contempt.
4 We've had more than enough
scorn from the arrogant
and contempt from the proud.

PSALM 126

ZION'S RESTORATION

A song of ascents.

1 When the LORD restored the fortunes of Zion,
we were like those who dream.
2 Our mouths were filled with laughter then,
and our tongues with shouts of joy.
Then they said among the nations,
"The LORD has done great things for them."
3 The LORD had done great things for us;
we were joyful.

4 Restore our fortunes, LORD,
like watercourses in the Negev.
5 Those who sow in tears
will reap with shouts of joy.
6 Though one goes along weeping,
carrying the bag of seed,
he will surely come back with shouts of joy,
carrying his sheaves.

PSALM 127

THE BLESSING OF THE LORD

A song of ascents. Of Solomon.

1 Unless the LORD builds a house,
its builders labor over it in vain;
unless the LORD watches over a city,
the watchman stays alert in vain.
2 In vain you get up early and stay up late,
working hard to have enough food—
yes, he gives sleep to the one he loves.

3 Sons are indeed a heritage from the LORD,
offspring, a reward.
4 Like arrows in the hand of a warrior
are the sons born in one's youth.
5 Happy is the man who has filled his quiver with them.
They will never be put to shame
when they speak with their enemies at the city gate.

PSALM 130

AWAITING REDEMPTION

A song of ascents.

1   Out of the depths I call to you, LORD!
2   Lord, listen to my voice;
    let your ears be attentive
    to my cry for help.

3   LORD, if you kept an account of iniquities,
    Lord, who could stand?
4   But with you there is forgiveness,
    so that you may be revered.

5   I wait for the LORD; I wait
    and put my hope in his word.
6   I wait for the Lord
    more than watchmen for the morning—
    more than watchmen for the morning.

7   Israel, put your hope in the LORD.
    For there is faithful love with the LORD,
    and with him is redemption in abundance.
8   And he will redeem Israel
    from all its iniquities.

PSALM 131

A CHILDLIKE SPIRIT

A song of ascents. Of David.

1   LORD, my heart is not proud;
    my eyes are not haughty.
    I do not get involved with things
    too great or too wondrous for me.
2   Instead, I have calmed and quieted my soul
    like a weaned child with its mother;
    my soul is like a weaned child.

3   Israel, put your hope in the LORD,
    both now and forever.

PSALM 139

THE ALL-KNOWING, EVER-PRESENT GOD

For the choir director. A psalm of David.

1 LORD, you have searched me and known me.
2 You know when I sit down and when I stand up;
you understand my thoughts from far away.
3 You observe my travels and my rest;
you are aware of all my ways.
4 Before a word is on my tongue,
you know all about it, LORD.
5 You have encircled me;
you have placed your hand on me.
6 This wondrous knowledge is beyond me.
It is lofty; I am unable to reach it.

7 Where can I go to escape your Spirit?
Where can I flee from your presence?
8 If I go up to heaven, you are there;
if I make my bed in Sheol, you are there.
9 If I fly on the wings of the dawn
and settle down on the western horizon,
10 even there your hand will lead me;
your right hand will hold on to me.
11 If I say, "Surely the darkness will hide me,
and the light around me will be night"—
12 even the darkness is not dark to you.
The night shines like the day;
darkness and light are alike to you.

13 For it was you who created my inward parts;
you knit me together in my mother's womb.
14 I will praise you
because I have been remarkably and
wondrously made.
Your works are wondrous,
and I know this very well.
15 My bones were not hidden from you
when I was made in secret,
when I was formed in the depths of the earth.
16 Your eyes saw me when I was formless;
all my days were written in your book and planned
before a single one of them began.

17 God, how precious your thoughts are to me;
how vast their sum is!
18 If I counted them,
they would outnumber the grains of sand;
when I wake up, I am still with you.

19 God, if only you would kill the wicked—
you bloodthirsty men, stay away from me—
20 who invoke you deceitfully.
Your enemies swear by you falsely.
21 LORD, don't I hate those who hate you,
and detest those who rebel against you?
22 I hate them with extreme hatred;
I consider them my enemies.

23 Search me, God, and know my heart;
test me and know my concerns.
24 See if there is any offensive way in me;
lead me in the everlasting way.

DAILY REFLECTION QUESTIONS

1   WHAT THEMES DID YOU NOTICE IN TODAY'S PSALMS?

2   WHAT METAPHORS, IMAGERY, OR POETIC DEVICES WERE
     USED IN TODAY'S PSALMS TO HIGHLIGHT THESE THEMES?

The Final

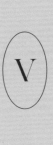

DAY 19

Hallelujah

PSALM 145

A hymn of David.

1   I exalt you, my God the King,
and bless your name forever and ever.

2   I will bless you every day;
I will praise your name forever and ever.

3   The LORD is great and is highly praised;
his greatness is unsearchable.

4   One generation will declare your works to the next
and will proclaim your mighty acts.

5   I will speak of your splendor and glorious majesty
and your wondrous works.

6   They will proclaim the power of your awe-inspiring acts,
and I will declare your greatness.

7   They will give a testimony of your great goodness
and will joyfully sing of your righteousness.

8   The LORD is gracious and compassionate,
slow to anger and great in faithful love.

9   The LORD is good to everyone;
his compassion rests on all he has made.

10   All you have made will thank you, LORD;
the faithful will bless you.

11   They will speak of the glory of your kingdom
and will declare your might,

12   informing all people of your mighty acts
and of the glorious splendor of your kingdom.

13   Your kingdom is an everlasting kingdom;
your rule is for all generations.
The LORD is faithful in all his words
and gracious in all his actions.

14   The LORD helps all who fall;
he raises up all who are oppressed.

15   All eyes look to you,
and you give them their food at the proper time.

16   You open your hand
and satisfy the desire of every living thing.

17   The LORD is righteous in all his ways
and faithful in all his acts.

Notes

¹⁸ The LORD is near all who call out to him,
all who call out to him with integrity.
¹⁹ He fulfills the desires of those who fear him;
he hears their cry for help and saves them.
²⁰ The LORD guards all those who love him,
but he destroys all the wicked.
²¹ My mouth will declare the LORD's praise;
let every living thing
bless his holy name forever and ever.

PSALMS 146–150

The Psalter closes with an extended section of unhindered praise.

PSALM 146

THE GOD OF COMPASSION

¹ Hallelujah!
My soul, praise the LORD.
² I will praise the LORD all my life;
I will sing to my God as long as I live.

³ Do not trust in nobles,
in a son of man, who cannot save.
⁴ When his breath leaves him,
he returns to the ground;
on that day his plans die.

⁵ Happy is the one whose help is the God of Jacob,
whose hope is in the LORD his God,
⁶ the Maker of heaven and earth,
the sea and everything in them.
He remains faithful forever,
⁷ executing justice for the exploited
and giving food to the hungry.
The LORD frees prisoners.
⁸ The LORD opens the eyes of the blind.
The LORD raises up those who are oppressed.
The LORD loves the righteous.
⁹ The LORD protects resident aliens
and helps the fatherless and the widow,
but he frustrates the ways of the wicked.

¹⁰ The LORD reigns forever;
Zion, your God reigns for all generations.
Hallelujah!

PSALM 147

GOD RESTORES JERUSALEM

1 Hallelujah!
How good it is to sing to our God,
for praise is pleasant and lovely.

2 The Lord rebuilds Jerusalem;
he gathers Israel's exiled people.

3 He heals the brokenhearted
and bandages their wounds.

4 He counts the number of the stars;
he gives names to all of them.

5 Our Lord is great, vast in power;
his understanding is infinite.

6 The Lord helps the oppressed
but brings the wicked to the ground.

7 Sing to the Lord with thanksgiving;
play the lyre to our God,

8 who covers the sky with clouds,
prepares rain for the earth,
and causes grass to grow on the hills.

9 He provides the animals with their food,
and the young ravens what they cry for.

10 He is not impressed by the strength of a horse;
he does not value the power of a warrior.

11 The Lord values those who fear him,
those who put their hope in his faithful love.

12 Exalt the Lord, Jerusalem;
praise your God, Zion!

13 For he strengthens the bars of your city gates
and blesses your children within you.

14 He endows your territory with prosperity;
he satisfies you with the finest wheat.

15 He sends his command throughout the earth;
his word runs swiftly.

16 He spreads snow like wool;
he scatters frost like ashes;

17 he throws his hailstones like crumbs.
Who can withstand his cold?

18 He sends his word and melts them;
he unleashes his winds, and the water flows.

19 He declares his word to Jacob,
his statutes and judgments to Israel.

20 He has not done this for every nation;
they do not know his judgments.
Hallelujah!

PSALM 148

CREATION'S PRAISE OF THE LORD

1 Hallelujah!
Praise the Lord from the heavens;
praise him in the heights.

2 Praise him, all his angels;
praise him, all his heavenly armies.

3 Praise him, sun and moon;
praise him, all you shining stars.

4 Praise him, highest heavens,
and you waters above the heavens.

5 Let them praise the name of the Lord,
for he commanded, and they were created.

6 He set them in position forever and ever;
he gave an order that will never pass away.

7 Praise the Lord from the earth,
all sea monsters and ocean depths,

8 lightning and hail, snow and cloud,
stormy wind that executes his command,

9 mountains and all hills,
fruit trees and all cedars,

10 wild animals and all cattle,
creatures that crawl and flying birds,

11 kings of the earth and all peoples,
princes and all judges of the earth,

12 young men as well as young women,
old and young together.

13 Let them praise the name of the Lord,
for his name alone is exalted.
His majesty covers heaven and earth.

¹⁴ He has raised up a horn for his people,
resulting in praise to all his faithful ones,
to the Israelites, the people close to him.
Hallelujah!

PSALM 149

PRAISE FOR GOD'S TRIUMPH

1 Hallelujah!
Sing to the LORD a new song,
his praise in the assembly of the faithful.
2 Let Israel celebrate its Maker;
let the children of Zion rejoice in their King.
3 Let them praise his name with dancing
and make music to him with tambourine and lyre.
4 For the LORD takes pleasure in his people;
he adorns the humble with salvation.
5 Let the faithful celebrate in triumphal glory;
let them shout for joy on their beds.

6 Let the exaltation of God be in their mouths
and a double-edged sword in their hands,
7 inflicting vengeance on the nations
and punishment on the peoples,
8 binding their kings with chains
and their dignitaries with iron shackles,
9 carrying out the judgment decreed against them.
This honor is for all his faithful people.
Hallelujah!

PSALM 150

PRAISE THE LORD

1 Hallelujah!
Praise God in his sanctuary.
Praise him in his mighty expanse.
2 Praise him for his powerful acts;
praise him for his abundant greatness.

3 Praise him with the blast of a ram's horn;
praise him with harp and lyre.
4 Praise him with tambourine and dance;
praise him with strings and flute.
5 Praise him with resounding cymbals;
praise him with clashing cymbals.

6 Let everything that breathes praise the LORD.
Hallelujah!

DAILY REFLECTION QUESTIONS

1   WHAT THEMES DID YOU NOTICE IN TODAY'S PSALMS?

2   WHAT METAPHORS, IMAGERY, OR POETIC DEVICES WERE
    USED IN TODAY'S PSALMS TO HIGHLIGHT THESE THEMES?

BOOK

V

Response

1

LOOK BACK AT YOUR DAILY REFLECTIONS. HOW DO EACH OF THE THEMES YOU NOTED CONTRIBUTE TO THE OVERALL MESSAGE OF BOOK V?
LOOK BACK AT PAGE 113 IF YOU NEED A REMINDER.

2

HOW DO THESE THEMES ANTICIPATE JESUS, THE ETERNAL KING?

3

HOW IS GOD DESCRIBED IN BOOK V?

4

WHAT DO THE PSALMS IN BOOK V MODEL FOR YOU AS A WORSHIPER?

Grace Day

· ·

Take this day to catch up on your reading, pray,
and rest in the presence of the Lord.

*For from him and through him
and to him are all things.
To him be the glory forever. Amen.*

ROMANS 11:36

Weekly
Truth

DAY 21

WWWWWWWWWWWWWWWWWWWWWWWWWWWWWWWWWWWWWWWWWWW

Scripture is God-breathed and true. When we memorize it, we carry His Word with us wherever we go.

For this reading plan, we've worked on memorizing Psalm 40:3. Spend some time today reviewing the full verse. Use this psalm as a reminder to respond to God with thanksgiving and praise.

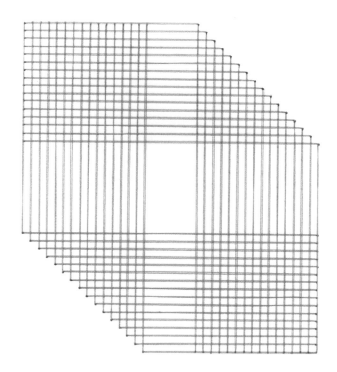

HE PUT A NEW SONG IN MY MOUTH,
A HYMN OF PRAISE TO OUR GOD.
MANY WILL SEE AND FEAR,
AND THEY WILL TRUST IN THE LORD.

PSALM 40:3

See tips for memorizing Scripture on page 144.

Benediction

From the mountaintop and from the deepest pit, we've read how we can join in the cries of God's people from generations past. From the groans of the exiles longing for restoration, to the call for a true and righteous King in Israel, to the final refrain of hallelujahs that close the Psalter, every psalm echoes a consistent hope. Every word, every emotion, every prayer, and every praise reflects worshipers who long for more. The book of Psalms expresses our longing for an eternal Savior.

And so we look ahead. While we join in the prayers and praise of God's people, we keep in view the true and better King they were waiting on. It is this Messiah, the King of kings, who would enter into the brokenness described in the Psalter. This King, the hope and answer to their prayers and ours, is Jesus. And His reign will never end.

Amen and amen!

He told them, "These are my words that I spoke to you while I was still with you—that everything written about me in the Law of Moses, the Prophets, and the Psalms must be fulfilled." Then he opened their minds to understand the Scriptures.

LUKE 24:44–45

Then I heard something like the voice of a vast multitude, like the sound of cascading waters, and like the rumbling of loud thunder, saying,

> Hallelujah, because our Lord God, the Almighty, reigns!
> Let us be glad, rejoice, and give him glory, because the marriage of the Lamb has come, and his bride has prepared herself.

REVELATION 19:6–7

Tips for Memorizing Scripture

At She Reads Truth, we believe Scripture memorization is an important discipline in your walk with God. Committing God's Truth to memory means He can minister to us—and we can minister to others—through His Word no matter where we are. As you approach the Weekly Truth passage in this book, try these memorization tips to see which techniques work best for you!

STUDY IT

Study the passage in its biblical context and ask yourself a few questions before you begin to memorize it: What does this passage say? What does it mean? How would I say this in my own words? What does it teach me about God? Understanding what the passage means helps you know why it is important to carry it with you wherever you go.

Break the passage into smaller sections, memorizing a phrase at a time.

PRAY IT

Use the passage you are memorizing as a prompt for prayer.

WRITE IT

Dedicate a notebook to Scripture memorization and write the passage over and over again.

Diagram the passage after you write it out. Place a square around the verbs, underline the nouns, and circle any adjectives or adverbs. Say the passage aloud several times, emphasizing the verbs as you repeat it. Then do the same thing again with the nouns, then the adjectives and adverbs.

Write out the first letter of each word in the passage somewhere you can reference it throughout the week as you work on your memorization.

Use a whiteboard to write out the passage. Erase a few words at a time as you continue to repeat it aloud. Keep erasing parts of the passage until you have it all committed to memory.

CREATE

If you can, make up a tune for the passage to sing as you go about your day, or try singing it to the tune of a favorite song.

Sketch the passage, visualizing what each phrase would look like in the form of a picture. Or, try using calligraphy or altering the style of your handwriting as you write it out.

Use hand signals or signs to come up with associations for each word or phrase and repeat the movements as you practice.

SAY IT

Repeat the passage out loud to yourself as you are going through the rhythm of your day—getting ready, pouring your coffee, waiting in traffic, or making dinner.

Listen to the passage read aloud to you.

Record a voice memo on your phone and listen to it throughout the day or play it on an audio Bible.

SHARE IT

Memorize the passage with a friend, family member, or mentor. Spontaneously challenge each other to recite the passage, or pick a time to review your passage and practice saying it from memory together.

Send the passage as an encouraging text to a friend, testing yourself as you type to see how much you have memorized so far.

KEEP AT IT!

Set reminders on your phone to prompt you to practice your passage.

Purchase a She Reads Truth 12 Card Set or keep a stack of notecards with Scripture you are memorizing by your bed. Practice reciting what you've memorized previously before you go to sleep, ending with the passages you are currently learning. If you wake up in the middle of the night, review them again instead of grabbing your phone. Read them out loud before you get out of bed in the morning.

Download the free Weekly Truth lock screens for your phone on the She Reads Truth app and read the passage throughout the day when you check your phone.

CSB BOOK ABBREVIATIONS

OLD TESTAMENT

GN Genesis	**JB** Job	**HAB** Habakkuk	**PHP** Philippians
EX Exodus	**PS** Psalms	**ZPH** Zephaniah	**COL** Colossians
LV Leviticus	**PR** Proverbs	**HG** Haggai	**1TH** 1 Thessalonians
NM Numbers	**EC** Ecclesiastes	**ZCH** Zechariah	**2TH** 2 Thessalonians
DT Deuteronomy	**SG** Song of Solomon	**MAL** Malachi	**1TM** 1 Timothy
JOS Joshua	**IS** Isaiah		**2TM** 2 Timothy
JDG Judges	**JR** Jeremiah	**NEW TESTAMENT**	**TI** Titus
RU Ruth	**LM** Lamentations	**MT** Matthew	**PHM** Philemon
1SM 1 Samuel	**EZK** Ezekiel	**MK** Mark	**HEB** Hebrews
2SM 2 Samuel	**DN** Daniel	**LK** Luke	**JMS** James
1KG 1 Kings	**HS** Hosea	**JN** John	**1PT** 1 Peter
2KG 2 Kings	**JL** Joel	**AC** Acts	**2PT** 2 Peter
1CH 1 Chronicles	**AM** Amos	**RM** Romans	**1JN** 1 John
2CH 2 Chronicles	**OB** Obadiah	**1CO** 1 Corinthians	**2JN** 2 John
EZR Ezra	**JNH** Jonah	**2CO** 2 Corinthians	**3JN** 3 John
NEH Nehemiah	**MC** Micah	**GL** Galatians	**JD** Jude
EST Esther	**NAH** Nahum	**EPH** Ephesians	**RV** Revelation

BIBLIOGRAPHY

Bullock, C. Hassell. *Encountering the Book of Psalms: A Literary and Theological Introduction.* Grand Rapids: Baker Academic, 2001.

DeClaissé-Walford, Nancy L., Rolf A. Jacobson, and Beth LaNeel Tanner. *The Book of Psalms.* The New International Commentary on the Old Testament. Grand Rapids: William B. Eerdmans Publishing Company, 2014.

Estes, Daniel J. *Handbook on the Wisdom Books and Psalms.* Grand Rapids: Baker Academic, 2005.

Kidner, Derek. *Psalms 73–150: An Introduction and Commentary.* Vol. 16. Tyndale Old Testament Commentaries. Downers Grove: InterVarsity Press, 1975.

Robertson, O. Palmer. *The Flow of the Psalms: Discovering Their Structure and Theology.* Phillipsburg: P&R Publishing, 2015.

Ross, Allen P. *A Commentary on the Psalms: Volume I (1–41).* Grand Rapids: Kregel Publications, 2011.

Ten Boom, Corrie, and Jamie Buckingham. *Tramp for the Lord.* Fort Washington: CLC Publications, 2011.

Wenham, Gordon. *The Psalter Reclaimed: Praying and Praising with the Psalms.* Wheaton: Crossway, 2013.

LOOKING FOR DEVOTIONALS?

Download the **She Reads Truth app** to find devotionals that complement your daily Scripture reading. If you're stuck on a passage, hop into the community discussion to connect with other Shes who are reading God's Word right along with you. You can also highlight Bible passages and download free lock screens for Weekly Truth memorization—all on the She Reads Truth app.

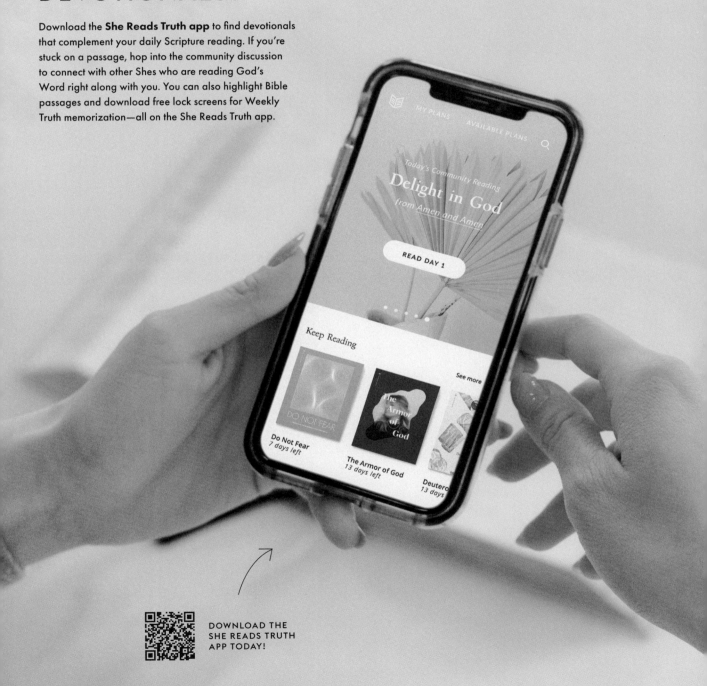

DOWNLOAD THE
SHE READS TRUTH
APP TODAY!

You just spent 21 days in the Word of God!

**MY FAVORITE DAY OF
THIS READING PLAN:**

**ONE THING I LEARNED
ABOUT GOD:**

**WHAT WAS GOD DOING IN
MY LIFE DURING THIS STUDY?**

HOW DID I FIND DELIGHT IN GOD'S WORD?

**WHAT DID I LEARN THAT I WANT TO SHARE
WITH SOMEONE ELSE?**

**A SPECIFIC SCRIPTURE THAT
ENCOURAGED ME:**

**A SPECIFIC SCRIPTURE THAT
CHALLENGED AND CONVICTED ME:**